FACTASTIC
BOOK OF
COMPARISONS

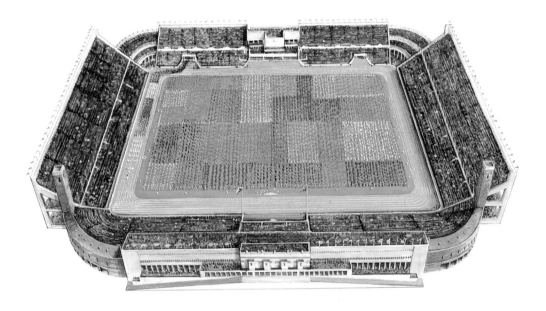

FACTASTIC
BOOK OF
COMPARISONS

RUSSELL ASH

[DK]

DORLING KINDERSLEY

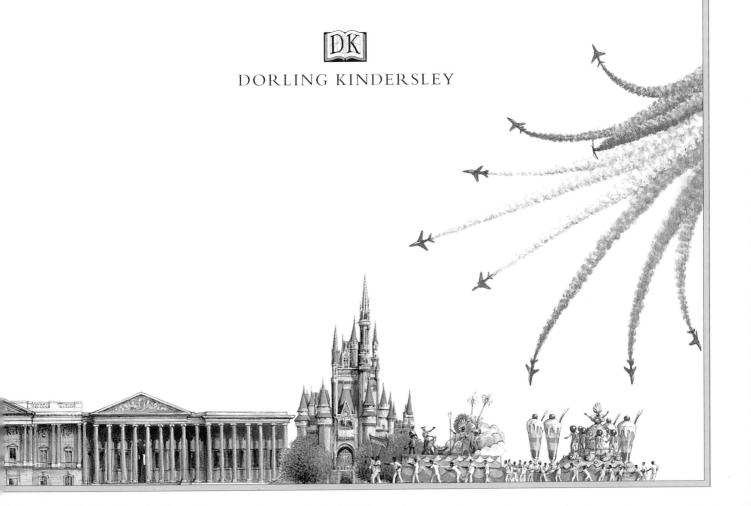

DK

A DORLING KINDERSLEY BOOK
www.dk.com

Art Editors Dominic Zwemmer,
Dorian Spencer Davies, Joanna Pocock
Project Editors Patrick Newman, Linda Sonntag
Editor Tim Hetherington
US Editor Camela Decaire
Senior Art Editor Dorian Spencer Davies
Senior Managing Art Editor Peter Bailey
Managing Editor Sarah Phillips
DTP Designer Karen Nettelfield
Production Charlotte Traill

Produced for Dorling Kindersley by
PAGE*One*, Cairn House,
Elgiva Lane, Chesham, Bucks, HP5 2JD

Published in the United States by Dorling Kindersley, Inc.,
95 Madison Avenue, New York, New York 10016

Text copyright © 1997 Russell Ash
Compilation and illustration copyright © 1997 Dorling Kindersley Limited, London

Part One first published as *Incredible Comparisons* in 1996;
Part Two first published as *The World in One Day* in 1997.
2 4 6 8 10 9 7 5 3 1

This version copyright © 1999 Dorling Kindersley Limited, London

A CIP catalog record is available
from the Library of Congress

ISBN 0-7894-5400-9

Reproduced in Great Britain by Dot Gradations Limited, Essex,
Printed and bound in Italy by L.E.G.O., Vicenza

The day featured throughout part two of this book is not any particular
one, but a typical day in the late 1990s. Of course, there may be certain
days when fewer babies are born, or more rice is harvested, for example,
but such figures, like all those that follow, are based on daily averages
that have been calculated from authoritative statistics for longer periods.

CONTENTS

PART ONE
INCREDIBLE COMPARISONS

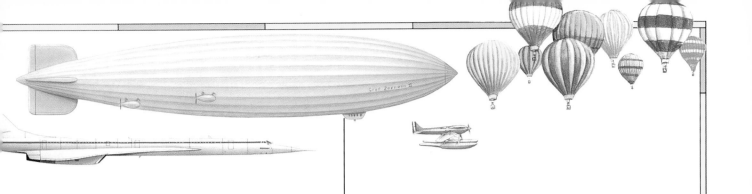

PART TWO
THE WORLD IN ONE DAY

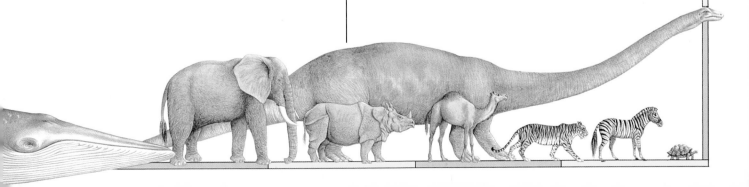

PART ONE
INCREDIBLE
COMPARISONS

HOW TO USE THIS PART

FROM AN EARLY AGE, people ask such questions as "How big is it?" or "How fast is it?" But even when we learn the answers, it is often hard to grasp what they really mean, especially when dealing with the extraordinary or the unfamiliar. We really want to know how things compare with the commonplace – with the weight of a human, the speed of a car, or the height of a house. *Incredible Comparisons* makes such relationships clear. While most of the comparisons are between real things, the illustrations allow visual comparisons that are impossible in real life. A mountain is turned upside down, vehicles from different ages come together in an amazing race, railroad tracks cross Mars – and the entire population of the world is invited to move to Bali. Turn the pages, and join in a fascinating exploration of a multitude of comparisons that reveal our world, and other worlds beyond, as never before.

TURNING THE PAGES

Each turn of a page will bring you to a new section on a new topic. Most sections consist of two pages, but some open out into four. The section shown here, on *Growth and age*, is two pages.

ABBREVIATIONS USED IN THIS PART

in	=	inch	km	=	kilometer
ft	=	foot	kph	=	kilometers per hour
mph	=	miles per hour	g	=	gram
oz	=	ounce	kg	=	kilogram
lb	=	pound	°F	=	degrees Fahrenheit
mm	=	millimeter	°C	=	degrees Celsius
cm	=	centimeter	sq	=	square
m	=	meter	%	=	percent

WEIGHTS AND MEASURES

1 ft	=	12 in
1 mile	=	5,280 ft
1 lb	=	16 oz
1 ton	=	2,000 lb
1 gallon	=	231 cubic in
1 cm	=	10 mm
1 m	=	100 cm
1 km	=	1,000 m
1 kg	=	1,000 g
1 tonne	=	1,000 kg
1 liter	=	1,000 cubic cm

LARGE NUMBERS

1,000,000	=	One million (One thousand thousand)
1,000,000,000	=	One billion (One thousand million)
1,000,000,000,000	=	One trillion (One million million)

Averaging people

Throughout this section, an average-size person of a certain age will be used as a standard for comparison. For example, the average two-year-old boy is 2 ft 9 in (84 cm) tall and weighs 26 lb (11.8 kg).

Personal point

Look for voice captions, which appear somewhere in nearly every section – you won't always be able to see who is doing the talking, but you will get an idea of your human size in comparison to the subject at hand.

For real

Many of the comparisons are real. This one shows a kind of deep-sea clam that takes 100 years to grow as big as your fingernail.

True size

Some things, such as this baby kangaroo, are shown actual size. A caption tells you when this is the case.

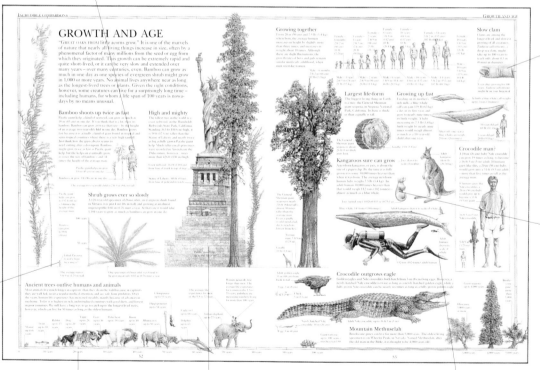

Scales of comparison

In nearly every section there is at least one horizontal or vertical scale, showing such things as the speed, size, and distance of various objects. This way you can make instant, at-a-glance comparisons between the different objects. The horizontal scale here shows how long various trees and animals live.

Moving from page to page

Several familiar objects are used as standards for comparison, such as the Statue of Liberty, shown here, and appear on different pages throughout. They allow you to make your own comparisons between objects on different pages.

Imaginary comparisons

Some of the comparisons are imaginary. For example, this shows that you would grow up to be as big as an adult blue whale if you grew at the same rate as a kangaroo.

Speed for speed

The French *TGV* train, the Concorde, and the X-15A-2 aircraft are among the vehicles that feature regularly in this section. In addition to straightforward speed comparisons, they are used to express long distances in terms of journey times.

French *TGV* train: fastest scheduled speed 158 mph (254.3 kph)

Concorde: cruising speed 1,354 mph (2,179 kph)

X-15A-2: maximum speed 4,534 mph (7,297 kph)

Square by square

Throughout, different surface areas are shown as squares. The larger the square, the bigger the surface area. In this example, the squares show the surface areas of different planets. Surface areas are also regularly compared with the area of one or more tennis courts.

Tennis court: 2,808 sq ft (261 sq m)

Neptune: surface area about 3,098,308,700 sq miles (8,024,000,000 sq km)

Uranus: surface area about 3,169,742,800 sq miles (8,209,000,000 sq km)

Saturn: surface area about 17,624,526,000 sq miles (45,644,000,000 sq km)

Jupiter: surface area about 25,113,522,000 sq miles (65,039,000,000 sq km)

By the tubful

Volumes of water and other liquids are sometimes given as the number of bathtubs they could fill.

Standard bathtub: 21 gallons (80 liters)

Very large volumes

Very large volumes – such as all the water in the Indian Ocean – are shown as cubes. The larger the cube, the bigger the volume.

Indian Ocean: 68,000,000 cubic miles (284,000,000 cubic km)

From place to place

Lengths and distances are often compared to the distances between cities. Here the Amazon River is compared to the distance between New York and Berlin.

New York

Berlin

Amazon River

Holding hands all in a line

Lengths and distances are also expressed by numbers of people holding hands. About 4 ft (1.2 m) is allowed for each person.

Great Wall of China

Height and depth

Buildings and other objects are used throughout to show heights and depths. Some of them are shown here.

Four-story town house: height 66 ft (20 m)

Empire State Building: height 1,250 ft (381 m)

Eiffel Tower: height 1,052 ft (321 m)

Saturn V rocket: height 364 ft (111 m)

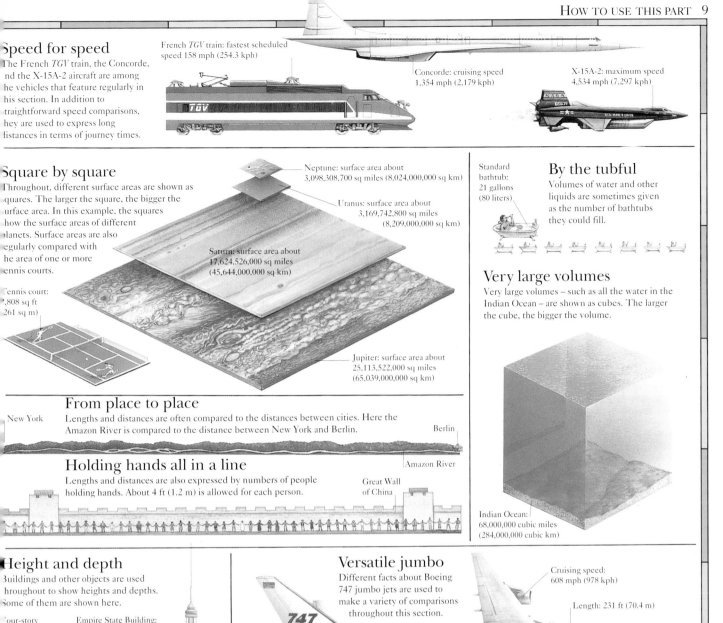

Versatile jumbo

Different facts about Boeing 747 jumbo jets are used to make a variety of comparisons throughout this section.

Cruising speed: 608 mph (978 kph)

Length: 231 ft (70.4 m)

Maximum passenger capacity: 570

Wingspan: 195.5 ft (59.6 m)

Thrust: 223,898 lb (101,560 kg)

Fuel capacity: 57,325 gallons (217,000 liters)

Weighty matters

The weights of different things are compared with the weights of a variety of objects, including a fully grown blue whale and an adult bull African elephant.

A fully grown blue whale may weigh 143 tons (130 tonnes) – or about as much as 26 adult bull African elephants.

An adult bull African elephant weighs about 5.5 tons (5 tonnes).

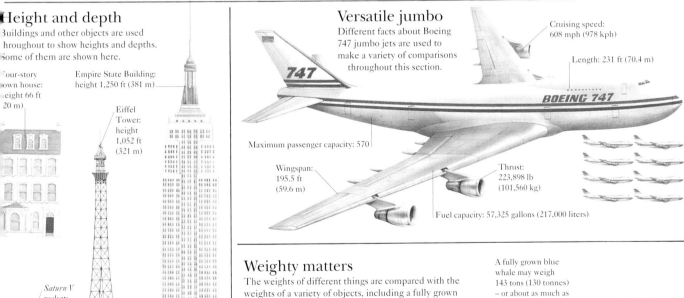

ON THE SURFACE

ALL THE LAND on Earth makes up only 29 percent of the planet's surface – the rest is sea. Three-quarters of all land is forest, desert, and pasture. Most of the rest is farmland, or is under ice. Mountains account for a very small area – towns and cities even less. If you scooped up the largest desert – the Sahara Desert, in northern Africa – and dumped it on the other side of the Atlantic Ocean, it would completely cover the continental US. Even the tallest skyscrapers would be buried under the massive sand dunes of the Sahara.

Turning forest into farmland

The surface area of Earth totals about 196,926,400 sq miles (510,000,000 sq km). Of that, just 57,610,626 sq miles (149,200,000 sq km) is land. After centuries of clearing trees – for timber, mining, and new farmland – forest still covers the largest part.

Forest	15,059,077 sq miles (39,000,000 sq km)	26 percent of total land area
Desert	13,630,396 sq miles (35,300,000 sq km)	24 percent of total land area
Pasture	13,205,652 sq miles (34,200,000 sq km)	23 percent of total land area
Icecap	5,791,953 sq miles (15,000,000 sq km)	10 percent of total land area
Cultivated	5,560,275 sq miles (14,400,000 sq km)	10 percent of total land area
Other	4,363,271 sq miles (11,300,000 sq km)	7 percent of total land area

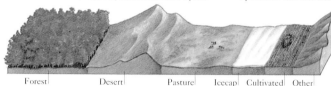

Forest · Desert · Pasture · Icecap · Cultivated · Other

Cross-country by TGV

Traveling at its fastest scheduled speed of 158 mph (254.3 kph), the French *TGV*, or High-Speed Train, would take under four hours to cover a distance equal to the widest part of its home country. It would take the same train almost 10 times as long, however, to cover a distance equal to the widest part of the largest country in the world, Russia.

France occupies an area of 198,857 sq miles (515,000 sq km). At its widest it measures 605 miles (974 km). The French *TGV* could cover this distance in just 3 hours and 58 minutes.

Vatican not so vast

A state within a state, the tiny Vatican City, in Italy, covers just 0.17 sq miles (0.44 sq km) – about the same area as 60 soccer fields, each being 328 ft (100 m) long and 239.5 ft (73 m) wide.

Outsized island

Greenland is the largest island on Earth, covering a total area of 840,065 sq miles (2,175,600 sq km). It is three times as big as Borneo, the second largest island in the world, and nine times as big as Honshu, the main island of Japan. Greenland belongs to Denmark, but if it were a separate country, it would actually be the thirteenth largest country in the world.

Honshu, Japan: 88,983 sq miles (230,448 sq km)

Borneo: 287,422 sq miles (744,366 sq km)

Greenland: 840,065 sq miles (2,175,600 sq km)

Covering an area of 967,570 sq miles (2,505,813 sq km), Sudan is the largest country in Africa. At its widest it measures 1,150 miles (1,850 km) – a distance equivalent to a *TGV* journey time of 7 hours and 31 minutes.

Australia covers 3,026,044 sq miles (7,836,848 sq km). At its widest it is 2,475 miles (3,983 km) from coast to coast. This is equivalent to a *TGV* journey time of 16 hours and 12 minutes.

I'm nearly there! If I were crossing Russia, however, I wouldn't even have reached the halfway point yet.

The total area of the US (including Alaska and Hawaii) is 3,679,459 sq miles (9,529,063 sq km). At its widest, the US is 2,807 miles (4,517 km) from coast to coast – equivalent to a *TGV* journey time of 18 hours and 22 minutes.

Russia is far and away the largest country on Earth, covering 6,593,328 sq miles (17,075,400 sq km). At its widest, Russia is a cross-country journey of 5,996 miles (9,650 km). It would take the *TGV* 39 hours and 14 minutes to cover this distance.

Unbroken border

The longest unbroken frontier in the world – between Canada and the US – stretches 3,987 miles (6,416 km). This is slightly longer than the Great Wall of China, which totals about 3,977 miles (6,400 km). Allowing about 4 ft (1.2 m) per person, this is equivalent to a line of some 5,300,000 people holding hands.

Fly me to the Moon

The total length of all the world's coastlines is not far short of the average distance between Earth and the Moon. Even at the Concorde's supersonic cruising speed of 1,354 mph (2,179 kph), it would take you a week to fly this far.

The total length of all the world's coastlines is reckoned to be about 221,214 miles (356,000 km).

Concorde

The average distance between Earth and the Moon is 238,613 miles (384,000 km).

The border between Canada and the US is longer than the Great Wall of China.

Each figure represents about 10,000 people.

A decade of deforestation

Clearing tropical rain forest causes loss of valuable plant and animal species, destruction of tribal peoples' ways of life, increased soil erosion, and possibly even global warming. Worldwide, in the 1980s some 585,027 sq miles (1,541,000 sq km) of rain forest were cleared – about 8 percent of the total.

Asia and the Pacific: 150,591 sq miles (390,000 sq km) of rain forest lost in the 1980s

Africa: 158,313 sq miles (410,000 sq km) lost in the 1980s

Overall, an area of rain forest larger than Alaska was cleared in the 1980s.

South America and the Caribbean: 286,122 sq miles (741,000 sq km) lost in the 1980s

Asia is biggest

Of the seven continents, the largest, Asia, accounts for almost a third of all the land on Earth.

Europe: 3,861,302 sq miles (10,000,000 sq km) – 7% of the world's land

Oceania: 3,475,172 sq miles (9,000,000 sq km) – 6% of the world's land

Antarctica: 5,405,823 sq miles (14,000,000 sq km) – 9.5% of the world's land

South America: 6,950,344 sq miles (18,000,000 sq km) – 12% of the world's land

North America: 9,267,125 sq miles (24,000,000 sq km) – 16% of the world's land

Africa: 11,583,906 sq miles (30,000,000 sq km) – 20% of the world's land

Asia: 16,989,728 sq miles (44,000,000 sq km) – 29.5% of the world's land

Desert lands that compare to whole countries

About a quarter of all land is desert. Some deserts are semi-arid. Other deserts are extremely arid, with almost no rainfall at all. The Australian Desert is bigger than India, yet it is less than half as big as the enormous Sahara Desert, in northern Africa.

The Kalahari Desert, in southern Africa, covers 200,788 sq miles (520,000 sq km) – an area bigger than France.

Covering 401,575 sq miles (1,040,000 sq km), the Gobi Desert is the largest desert in Asia.

At 501,969 sq miles (1,300,000 sq km), the Arabian Desert is bigger than Peru.

The Australian Desert covers 1,467,295 sq miles (3,800,000 sq km).

The Sahara Desert is the largest desert in the world, covering 3,500,270 sq miles (9,065,000 sq km).

Mountains of desert sand

The world's tallest sand dunes are found in the Sahara. They are big enough to bury big buildings such as the Great Pyramid, in Egypt, and the Eiffel Tower, in Paris.

Some sand dunes in the African Sahara are 1,526 ft (465 m) tall – more than 23 times as tall as a four-story town house.

Four-story town house: 66 ft (20 m)

Eiffel Tower: 1,052 ft (321 m)

Great Pyramid: 481 ft (147 m)

An Eiffel lot of ice

The icecap over the South Pole is 9,186 ft (2,800 m) thick – almost as deep as a stack of nine Eiffel Towers. Incredibly, in some places the Antarctic icecap is 15,682 ft (4,780 m) thick – almost as deep as 15 Eiffel Towers.

Icecap over South Pole: 9,186 ft (2,800 m)

Nine Eiffel Towers: 9,478 ft (2,889 m)

A desert as big as the US

The Sahara Desert extends across northern Africa. With large expanses receiving little or no rain for years at a time, and an average annual temperature of 80°F (27°C), it is an inhospitable region supporting fewer than 2,000,000 people, mostly on its relatively fertile margins. The Sahara covers an area about the size of the continental US. The population of the US is more than 130 times as big, however. Only three countries in the world are bigger than the Sahara Desert: Russia, Canada, and China.

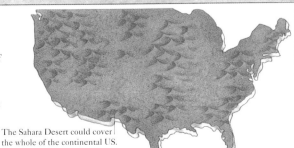

The Sahara Desert could cover the whole of the continental US.

3,728 miles (6,000 km)   4,350 miles (7,000 km)   4,971 miles (8,000 km)   5,592 miles (9,000 km)   6,214 miles (10,000 km)

INTO THE EARTH

VIEWED FROM SPACE through the window of an orbiting spacecraft, the Earth appears to be completely smooth, like a multicolored beachball. Yet the surface of our planet is pitted with craters, scored with canyons, and riddled with caves. The deepest hole ever drilled is deeper than the deepest canyon – but it does not even break through the Earth's crust, which covers the interior of the planet like the skin of a giant apple.

Colossal craters

Sudbury Crater, in Ontario, Canada, is 87 miles (140 km) wide. It is the largest crater on Earth. There are much bigger craters on the Moon, however – all of them made by meteorites. Bailly Crater, for example, is nearly as wide as the distance from Paris to London.

London

Bailly Crater is the largest crater on the near side of the Moon. On the dark side, however, the Orientale Basin is three times as large.

Chasmic canyons

Canyons are very deep, very narrow valleys, with very steep – almost vertical – sides. They are usually found in hot, dry places, where soft or weak rock is rapidly worn through by rivers, but where there is not enough rain to wash away the sides of the river valleys. The great canyons of the US are the most spectacular of all. At its deepest point, Kings Canyon, in California, is deep enough to swallow a stack of six-and-a-half Empire State Buildings.

Empire State Building, New York: 1,250 ft (381 m) tall

The Snake River has gouged out Hells Canyon, in Oregon and Idaho, to a maximum depth of 7,900 ft (2,408 m) – more than three-and-a-half times as deep as the deepest point in the North Sea.

Kings Canyon: maximum depth 8,199 ft (2,499 m)

Caves top canyons

One of the true wonders of the natural world, the mighty Grand Canyon is more than twice as long as Hells Canyon and nine times as long as Kings Canyon. The combined length of all the caves in the Mammoth Cave system, in Kentucky, is even greater, however.

Hello, down there! I'm nearly halfway down, but I'm still more than three times as high up as the top of the Empire State Building.

Solid as a rock?

The Earth's crust consists of solid rock, but if you were to break it down into its component elements, nearly half of it would vanish into thin air! This is because almost half of the Earth's crust is made up of just one element – oxygen.

Oxygen: 46.6%

Silicon: 27.7%

Aluminum: 8.1%

The Grand Canyon, in Arizona, was formed by the Colorado River, and has a maximum depth of 5,249 ft (1,600 m) – equivalent to a stack of 80 four-story town houses.

Sodium: 2.8%

Iron: 5%
Calcium: 3.6%
Potassium: 2.6%
Magnesium: 2.1%
Hydrogen: 1%
Titanium: 0.5%

The North Sea has a maximum depth of 2,165 ft (660 m). Its average depth, however, is only 308 ft (94 m).

Kings Canyon is in the Sierra Nevada mountains. Unlike Hells Canyon and the Grand Canyon, which were formed solely by river erosion, Kings Canyon was formed by a combination of river erosion and erosion by glaciers.

Four-story town house 66 ft (20 m)

9,843 ft (3,000 m)

8,202 ft (2,500 m)

6,562 ft (2,000 m)

4,921 ft (1,500 m)

3,281 ft (1,000 m)

1,640 ft (500 m)

0

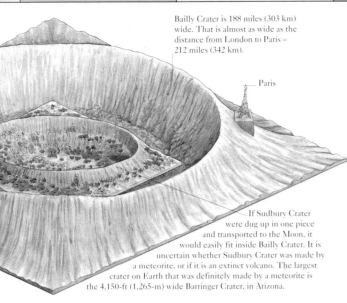

Bailly Crater is 188 miles (303 km) wide. That is almost as wide as the distance from London to Paris – 212 miles (342 km).

Paris

If Sudbury Crater were dug up in one piece and transported to the Moon, it would easily fit inside Bailly Crater. It is uncertain whether Sudbury Crater was made by a meteorite, or if it is an extinct volcano. The largest crater on Earth that was definitely made by a meteorite is the 4,150-ft (1,265-m) wide Barringer Crater, in Arizona.

Borehole barely pricks the skin

The average distance to the center of the Earth is 3,963 miles (6,378 km). On average, the crust is 15 miles (24 km) thick. The deepest hole ever drilled – at Kola Peninsula, in Russia – is about 7.5 miles (12 km) deep. If the Earth was an apple and the crust its skin, this hole would not even pierce the skin.

The Kola Peninsula borehole is one-and-a-half times as deep as Mt. Everest is high, but does not even break through the Earth's crust.

The thickness of the Earth's crust varies from 3 miles (5 km) in places under the sea to 37 miles (60 km) below some mountains.

Upper mantle: mostly solid, with a liquid layer

The lower mantle is solid.

The outer core is molten metal.

The inner core is a solid ball of intensely hot iron under extreme pressure.

0
9,843 ft (3,000 m)
19,685 ft (6,000 m)
29,528 ft (9,000 m)
39,370 ft (12,000 m)
49,213 ft (15,000 m)

Western Deep Levels gold mine, South Africa: 12,392 ft (3,777 m)

Oil boreholes rarely extend deeper than 29,856 ft (9,100 m).

In 1970, a geological survey team began to bore a hole at the Kola Peninsula. By April 1992, it was 40,230 ft (12,262 m) deep.

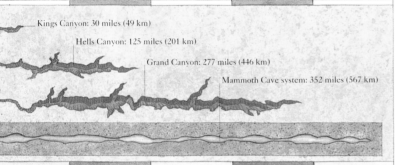

75 miles (120 km)   149 miles (240 km)   224 miles (360 km)   298 miles (480 km)

Kings Canyon: 30 miles (49 km)

Hells Canyon: 125 miles (201 km)

Grand Canyon: 277 miles (446 km)

Mammoth Cave system: 352 miles (567 km)

75 miles (120 km)   149 miles (240 km)   224 miles (360 km)   298 miles (480 km)

How low can you go?

Some places on Earth lie below sea level, the average level of the surface of the oceans. These depressions usually result from deformations or folds in the Earth's crust.

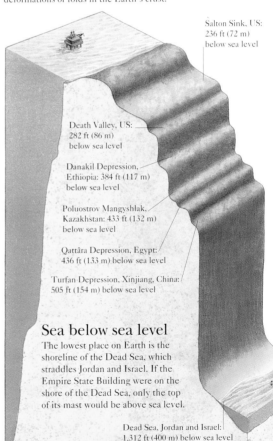

Salton Sink, US: 236 ft (72 m) below sea level

Death Valley, US: 282 ft (86 m) below sea level

Danakil Depression, Ethiopia: 384 ft (117 m) below sea level

Poluostrov Mangyshlak, Kazakhstan: 433 ft (132 m) below sea level

Qattâra Depression, Egypt: 436 ft (133 m) below sea level

Turfan Depression, Xinjiang, China: 505 ft (154 m) below sea level

Sea below sea level

The lowest place on Earth is the shoreline of the Dead Sea, which straddles Jordan and Israel. If the Empire State Building were on the shore of the Dead Sea, only the top of its mast would be above sea level.

Dead Sea, Jordan and Israel: 1,312 ft (400 m) below sea level

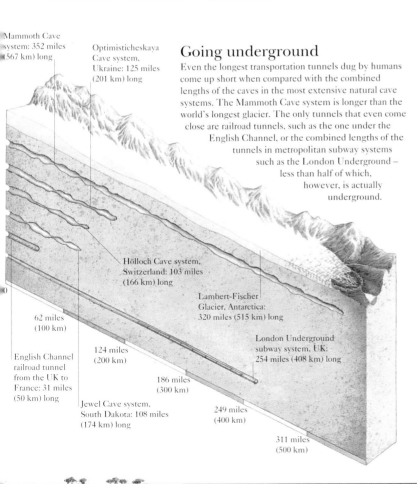

Mammoth Cave system: 352 miles (567 km) long

Optimisticheskaya Cave system, Ukraine: 125 miles (201 km) long

Going underground

Even the longest transportation tunnels dug by humans come up short when compared with the combined lengths of the caves in the most extensive natural cave systems. The Mammoth Cave system is longer than the world's longest glacier. The only tunnels that even come close are railroad tunnels, such as the one under the English Channel, or the combined lengths of the tunnels in metropolitan subway systems such as the London Underground – less than half of which, however, is actually underground.

Hölloch Cave system, Switzerland: 103 miles (166 km) long

Lambert-Fischer Glacier, Antarctica: 320 miles (515 km) long

London Underground subway system, UK: 254 miles (408 km) long

62 miles (100 km)

English Channel railroad tunnel from the UK to France: 31 miles (50 km) long

124 miles (200 km)

Jewel Cave system, South Dakota: 108 miles (174 km) long

186 miles (300 km)

249 miles (400 km)

311 miles (500 km)

GOING INTO SPACE

"THREE... TWO... ONE... We have liftoff!" Your seat vibrates and you start moving upward, slowly at first, then ever faster. You are on board the world's most powerful vehicle, being thrust into space with the force of 31 jumbo jets. The ride is surprisingly smooth, however – some roller-coasters push you harder into your seat – so you hardly realize you are traveling 10 times faster than a rifle bullet. In orbit, you have a unique view of Earth, floating in the vastness of space. With luck, you might spot a mighty comet the size of France, with a tail as long as five planets. But watch out for meteorites. At orbital velocity, a plum-sized meteorite can do as much damage as a speeding car.

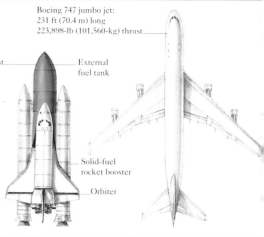

Wind speeds on Neptune, which has an atmosphere of mainly hydrogen, reach 1,243 mph (2,000 kph) – 10 times as fast as the strongest tropical storms on Earth.

| 0 | 932 mph (1,500 kph) | 3,107 mph (5,000 kph) |

The speed of sound through air at ground level on Earth is 764 mph (1,229 kph).

Space is the place for speed

Friction restricts the speed of objects through air. But space is a near vacuum, so probes such as *Helios B* can travel many times faster than any object through air. Even the planets move at high speeds as they orbit the Sun. The only thing that travels faster through air than through space is sound. The speed of sound in space zero, because sound cannot travel in a vacuum – space is completely silent.

Cargo space

A space shuttle has a cargo bay big enough to hold a humpback whale – with room to spare for 1,000 or so herrings. Alternatively, you could fill it with 250,000 4-oz (118-g) chocolate candy bars.

The cargo bay of a space shuttle is 60 ft (18.3 m) long and can hold up to 33 tons (29.5 tonnes). A fully grown humpback whale is about 49 ft (15 m) long and weighs about 32 tons (29 tonnes).

Standing tall on the launch pad

Launchers at the Kennedy Space Center, at Cape Canaveral, Florida, tower over the marshland surrounding the complex. *Saturn V* rockets, which were used for the *Apollo* Moon missions in the 1960s and early 1970s, were as tall as a 30-story building. At liftoff, even a space shuttle is as tall as the Leaning Tower of Pisa, in Italy.

Saturn V rocket (1973): 364 ft (111 m)

361 ft (110 m)
328 ft (100 m)
295 ft (90 m)
262 ft (80 m)
230 ft (70 m)
197 ft (60 m)
164 ft (50 m)
131 ft (40 m)
98 ft (30 m)
66 ft (20 m)
33 ft (10 m)
0

Shuttle power

At liftoff, a space shuttle comprises a huge external fuel tank and two solid-fuel rocket boosters as well as the familiar orbiter. It is almost 31 times as powerful as a Boeing 747 jumbo jet. This is because a space shuttle must quickly accelerate to a staggering 17,400 mph (28,000 kph) – nearly four times as fast as the world's fastest plane, the X-15A-2 – to get into orbit above the Earth's atmosphere.

31 jumbo jets: combined thrust 6,940,829 lb (3,148,360 kg)

Space shuttle at liftoff: 184 ft (56 m) tall 6,924,427-lb (3,140,920-kg) thrust

Boeing 747 jumbo jet: 231 ft (70.4 m) long 223,898-lb (101,560-kg) thrust

External fuel tank

Solid-fuel rocket booster

Orbiter

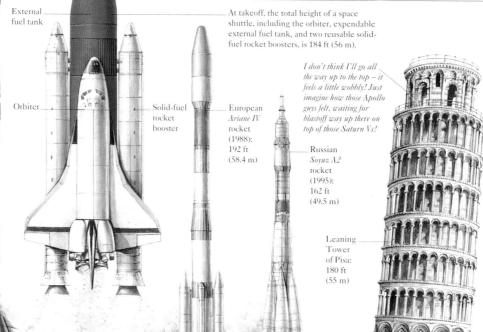

External fuel tank

Orbiter

Solid-fuel rocket booster

European *Ariane IV* rocket (1988): 192 ft (58.4 m)

Russian *Soyuz A2* rocket (1995): 162 ft (49.5 m)

At takeoff, the total height of a space shuttle, including the orbiter, expendable external fuel tank, and two reusable solid-fuel rocket boosters, is 184 ft (56 m).

I don't think I'll go all the way up to the top – it feels a little wobbly! Just imagine how those Apollo guys felt, waiting for blastoff way up there on top of those Saturn Vs!

Leaning Tower of Pisa: 180 ft (55 m)

Compact probe

Space capsules, satellites, and probes are tiny compared to the powerful rocket and shuttle launchers that propel them out of the Earth's atmosphere and into space. The *Giotto* space probe, which flew past Halley's Comet in 1986, was about the same size as a small car.

Giotto space probe: 10 ft (3.1 m)

Collision course

Giotto scientists knew that debris pouring off Halley's Comet would eventually destroy the probe – but not before it had beamed invaluabl photographs and data back to Earth

Giotto: 10 ft (3.1 m)

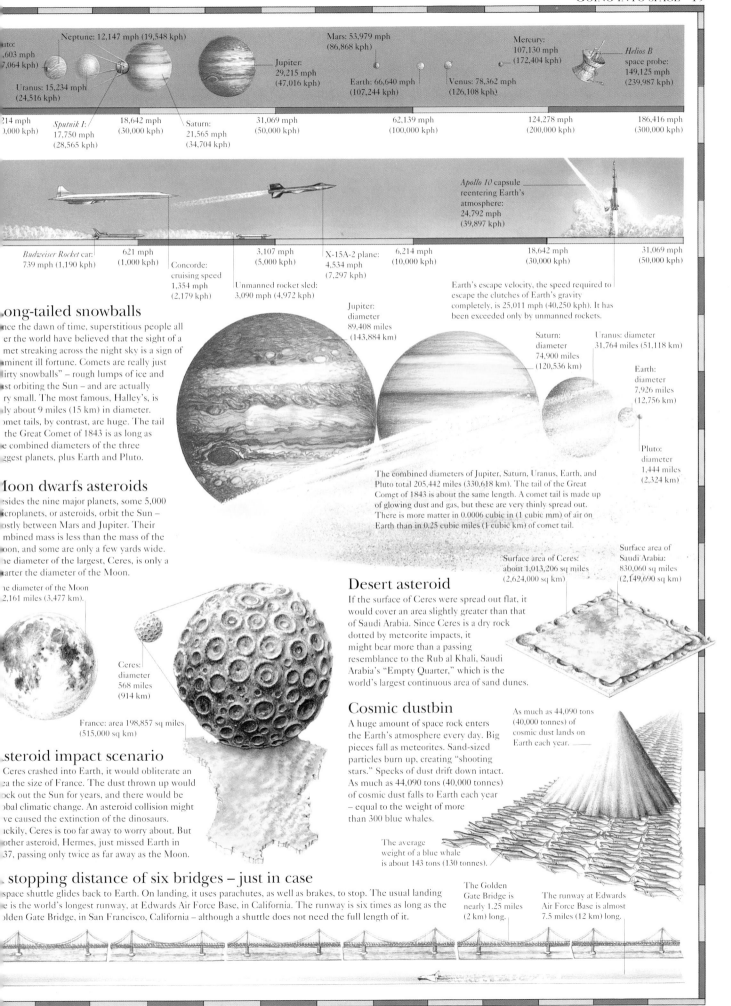

...uto:
...,603 mph
...,064 kph)

Neptune: 12,147 mph (19,548 kph)

Uranus: 15,234 mph (24,516 kph)

Mars: 53,979 mph (86,868 kph)

Jupiter: 29,215 mph (47,016 kph)

Earth: 66,640 mph (107,244 kph)

Venus: 78,362 mph (126,108 kph)

Mercury: 107,130 mph (172,404 kph)

Helios B space probe: 149,125 mph (239,987 kph)

...214 mph
...,000 kph)

Sputnik I: 17,750 mph (28,565 kph)

18,642 mph (30,000 kph)

Saturn: 21,565 mph (34,704 kph)

31,069 mph (50,000 kph)

62,139 mph (100,000 kph)

124,278 mph (200,000 kph)

186,416 mph (300,000 kph)

Apollo 10 capsule reentering Earth's atmosphere: 24,792 mph (39,897 kph)

Budweiser Rocket car: 739 mph (1,190 kph)

621 mph (1,000 kph)

Concorde: cruising speed 1,354 mph (2,179 kph)

3,107 mph (5,000 kph)

Unmanned rocket sled: 3,090 mph (4,972 kph)

X-15A-2 plane: 4,534 mph (7,297 kph)

6,214 mph (10,000 kph)

18,642 mph (30,000 kph)

31,069 mph (50,000 kph)

Earth's escape velocity, the speed required to escape the clutches of Earth's gravity completely, is 25,011 mph (40,250 kph). It has been exceeded only by unmanned rockets.

Long-tailed snowballs

...nce the dawn of time, superstitious people all ...er the world have believed that the sight of a ...met streaking across the night sky is a sign of ...minent ill fortune. Comets are really just ...irty snowballs" – rough lumps of ice and ...st orbiting the Sun – and are actually ...ry small. The most famous, Halley's, is ...ly about 9 miles (15 km) in diameter. ...omet tails, by contrast, are huge. The tail ...the Great Comet of 1843 is as long as ...e combined diameters of the three ...ggest planets, plus Earth and Pluto.

Jupiter: diameter 89,408 miles (143,884 km)

Saturn: diameter 74,900 miles (120,536 km)

Uranus: diameter 31,764 miles (51,118 km)

Earth: diameter 7,926 miles (12,756 km)

Pluto: diameter 1,444 miles (2,324 km)

The combined diameters of Jupiter, Saturn, Uranus, Earth, and Pluto total 205,442 miles (330,618 km). The tail of the Great Comet of 1843 is about the same length. A comet tail is made up of glowing dust and gas, but these are very thinly spread out. There is more matter in 0.0006 cubic in (1 cubic mm) of air on Earth than in 0.25 cubic miles (1 cubic km) of comet tail.

Moon dwarfs asteroids

...esides the nine major planets, some 5,000 ...icroplanets, or asteroids, orbit the Sun – ...ostly between Mars and Jupiter. Their ...mbined mass is less than the mass of the ...oon, and some are only a few yards wide. ...e diameter of the largest, Ceres, is only a ...arter the diameter of the Moon.

...e diameter of the Moon ...2,161 miles (3,477 km).

Ceres: diameter 568 miles (914 km)

France: area 198,857 sq miles (515,000 sq km)

Surface area of Ceres: about 1,013,206 sq miles (2,624,000 sq km)

Surface area of Saudi Arabia: 830,060 sq miles (2,149,690 sq km)

Desert asteroid

If the surface of Ceres were spread out flat, it would cover an area slightly greater than that of Saudi Arabia. Since Ceres is a dry rock dotted by meteorite impacts, it might bear more than a passing resemblance to the Rub al Khali, Saudi Arabia's "Empty Quarter," which is the world's largest continuous area of sand dunes.

Asteroid impact scenario

...Ceres crashed into Earth, it would obliterate an ...ea the size of France. The dust thrown up would ...ock out the Sun for years, and there would be ...obal climatic change. An asteroid collision might ...ve caused the extinction of the dinosaurs. ...uckily, Ceres is too far away to worry about. But ...other asteroid, Hermes, just missed Earth in ...37, passing only twice as far away as the Moon.

Cosmic dustbin

A huge amount of space rock enters the Earth's atmosphere every day. Big pieces fall as meteorites. Sand-sized particles burn up, creating "shooting stars." Specks of dust drift down intact. As much as 44,090 tons (40,000 tonnes) of cosmic dust falls to Earth each year – equal to the weight of more than 300 blue whales.

As much as 44,090 tons (40,000 tonnes) of cosmic dust lands on Earth each year.

The average weight of a blue whale is about 143 tons (130 tonnes).

A stopping distance of six bridges – just in case

...space shuttle glides back to Earth. On landing, it uses parachutes, as well as brakes, to stop. The usual landing ...e is the world's longest runway, at Edwards Air Force Base, in California. The runway is six times as long as the ...olden Gate Bridge, in San Francisco, California – although a shuttle does not need the full length of it.

The Golden Gate Bridge is nearly 1.25 miles (2 km) long.

The runway at Edwards Air Force Base is almost 7.5 miles (12 km) long.

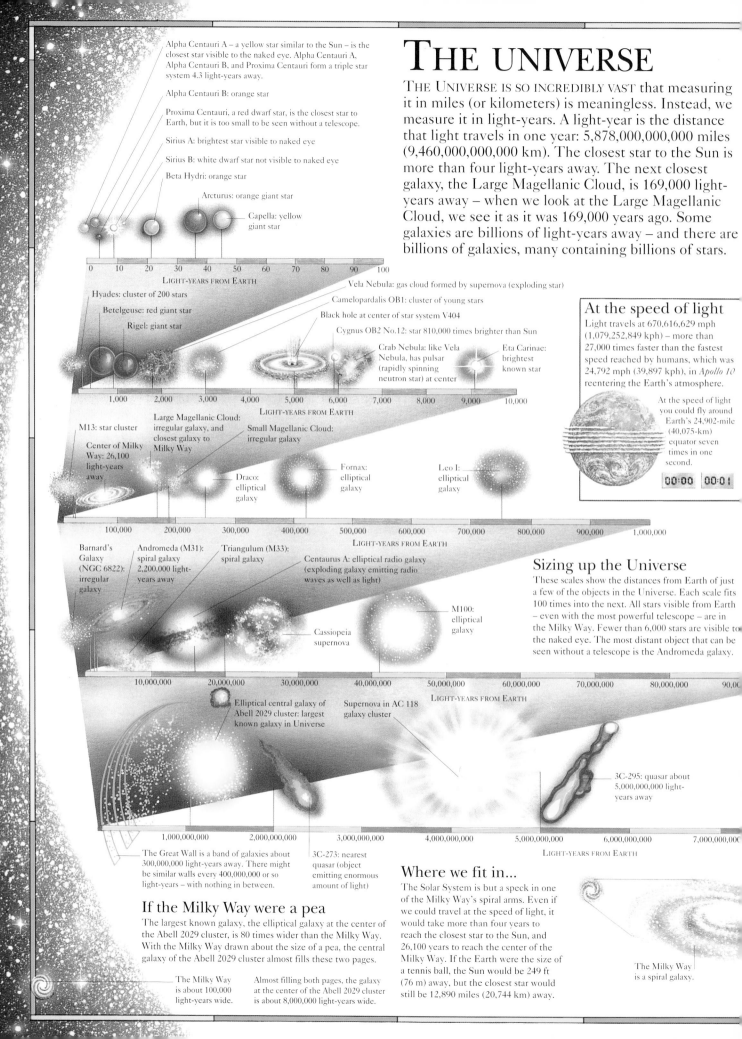

THE UNIVERSE

THE UNIVERSE IS SO INCREDIBLY VAST that measuring it in miles (or kilometers) is meaningless. Instead, we measure it in light-years. A light-year is the distance that light travels in one year: 5,878,000,000,000 miles (9,460,000,000,000 km). The closest star to the Sun is more than four light-years away. The next closest galaxy, the Large Magellanic Cloud, is 169,000 light-years away – when we look at the Large Magellanic Cloud, we see it as it was 169,000 years ago. Some galaxies are billions of light-years away – and there are billions of galaxies, many containing billions of stars.

Alpha Centauri A – a yellow star similar to the Sun – is the closest star visible to the naked eye. Alpha Centauri A, Alpha Centauri B, and Proxima Centauri form a triple star system 4.3 light-years away.

Alpha Centauri B: orange star

Proxima Centauri, a red dwarf star, is the closest star to Earth, but it is too small to be seen without a telescope.

Sirius A: brightest star visible to naked eye

Sirius B: white dwarf star not visible to naked eye

Beta Hydri: orange star

Arcturus: orange giant star

Capella: yellow giant star

LIGHT-YEARS FROM EARTH
0 10 20 30 40 50 60 70 80 90 100

Hyades: cluster of 200 stars

Betelgeuse: red giant star

Rigel: giant star

Vela Nebula: gas cloud formed by supernova (exploding star)

Camelopardalis OB1: cluster of young stars

Black hole at center of star system V404

Cygnus OB2 No.12: star 810,000 times brighter than Sun

Crab Nebula: like Vela Nebula, has pulsar (rapidly spinning neutron star) at center

Eta Carinae: brightest known star

LIGHT-YEARS FROM EARTH
1,000 2,000 3,000 4,000 5,000 6,000 7,000 8,000 9,000 10,000

At the speed of light
Light travels at 670,616,629 mph (1,079,252,849 kph) – more than 27,000 times faster than the fastest speed reached by humans, which was 24,792 mph (39,897 kph), in *Apollo 10* reentering the Earth's atmosphere.

At the speed of light you could fly around Earth's 24,902-mile (40,075-km) equator seven times in one second.

00:00 00:01

M13: star cluster

Center of Milky Way: 26,100 light-years away

Large Magellanic Cloud: irregular galaxy, and closest galaxy to Milky Way

Small Magellanic Cloud: irregular galaxy

Draco: elliptical galaxy

Fornax: elliptical galaxy

Leo I: elliptical galaxy

LIGHT-YEARS FROM EARTH
100,000 200,000 300,000 400,000 500,000 600,000 700,000 800,000 900,000 1,000,000

Barnard's Galaxy (NGC 6822): irregular galaxy

Andromeda (M31): spiral galaxy 2,200,000 light-years away

Triangulum (M33): spiral galaxy

Centaurus A: elliptical radio galaxy (exploding galaxy emitting radio waves as well as light)

Cassiopeia supernova

M100: elliptical galaxy

Sizing up the Universe
These scales show the distances from Earth of just a few of the objects in the Universe. Each scale fits 100 times into the next. All stars visible from Earth – even with the most powerful telescope – are in the Milky Way. Fewer than 6,000 stars are visible to the naked eye. The most distant object that can be seen without a telescope is the Andromeda galaxy.

LIGHT-YEARS FROM EARTH
10,000,000 20,000,000 30,000,000 40,000,000 50,000,000 60,000,000 70,000,000 80,000,000 90,00

Elliptical central galaxy of Abell 2029 cluster: largest known galaxy in Universe

Supernova in AC 118 galaxy cluster

3C-295: quasar about 5,000,000,000 light-years away

LIGHT-YEARS FROM EARTH
1,000,000,000 2,000,000,000 3,000,000,000 4,000,000,000 5,000,000,000 6,000,000,000 7,000,000,00

The Great Wall is a band of galaxies about 300,000,000 light-years away. There might be similar walls every 400,000,000 or so light-years – with nothing in between.

3C-273: nearest quasar (object emitting enormous amount of light)

Where we fit in...
The Solar System is but a speck in one of the Milky Way's spiral arms. Even if we could travel at the speed of light, it would take more than four years to reach the closest star to the Sun, and 26,100 years to reach the center of the Milky Way. If the Earth were the size of a tennis ball, the Sun would be 249 ft (76 m) away, but the closest star would still be 12,890 miles (20,744 km) away.

The Milky Way is a spiral galaxy.

If the Milky Way were a pea
The largest known galaxy, the elliptical galaxy at the center of the Abell 2029 cluster, is 80 times wider than the Milky Way. With the Milky Way drawn about the size of a pea, the central galaxy of the Abell 2029 cluster almost fills these two pages.

The Milky Way is about 100,000 light-years wide.

Almost filling both pages, the galaxy at the center of the Abell 2029 cluster is about 8,000,000 light-years wide.

Big Betelgeuse

Stars come in many different sizes. Compared with some stars, the Sun is enormous. Compared with others, it is tiny. The largest known star is the red giant Betelgeuse, some 310 light-years away. The diameter of Betelgeuse is about 500 times greater than the diameter of the Sun. If Betelgeuse were the size of a large orange, the Sun would be about the size of the head of a pin.

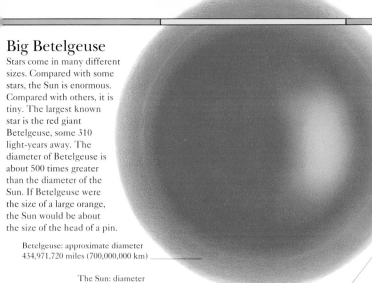

Betelgeuse: approximate diameter 434,971,720 miles (700,000,000 km)

The Sun: diameter 865,059 miles (1,392,140 km)

A midget among stars

Stars such as the Sun eventually turn into white dwarfs, which are very small, but extremely dense, stars. The Sun is about 250 times wider than the smallest known white dwarf, L362-81, which is almost as small as the Moon.

Earth: diameter 7,926 miles (12,756 km)

The Moon: diameter 2,161 miles (3,477 km)

L362-81: estimated diameter 3,480 miles (5,600 km)

The Sun at the same scale as Earth, L362-81, and the Moon

Core cauldron

Like most stars, the Sun is a huge ball of glowing hydrogen. At the Sun's core, the pressure and temperature are so great that hydrogen atoms fuse to make helium. Every second, at its core, the Sun converts about 595,247,400 tons (540,000,000 tonnes) of hydrogen into helium – a weight equal to about 103.5 Great Pyramids.

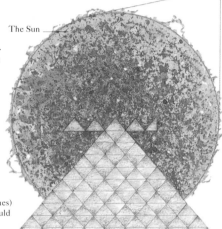

The Sun

The Great Pyramid weighs 5,750,090 tons (5,216,400 tonnes) – so 103.5 Great Pyramids would weigh 595,134,303 tons (539,897,400 tonnes).

Pincredibly dense

Massive stars such as Betelgeuse eventually turn into neutron stars, which are even smaller and denser than white dwarf stars. A neutron star is so dense that just a pinhead-sized amount of one might weigh as much as three Empire State Buildings.

The Empire State Building weighs 365,000 tons (331,122 tonnes) – so three Empire State Buildings would weigh 1,095,000 tons (993,366 tonnes).

A pinhead-sized piece of a neutron star might weigh 1,102,310 tons (1,000,000 tonnes).

Siriusly heavy

The diameter of the Sun is 144 times greater than the diameter of the white dwarf star Sirius B, which is even smaller than Earth. Sirius B is so dense, however, that it actually weighs more than the Sun, which is itself some 330,000 times heavier than Earth.

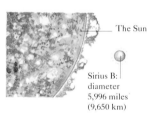

The Sun

Sirius B: diameter 5,996 miles (9,650 km)

100,000,000

G2237+0305: quasar

IRAS F10214+4724 is an object 300,000,000,000,000 times brighter than the Sun. It is probably a galaxy.

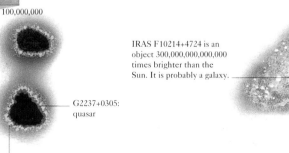

Some 12,800,000,000 light-years distant, radio source 4C41.17 is the remotest known galaxy in the Universe.

PC 1247+3406, a quasar, is about 13,200,000,000 light-years away, making it the remotest known object in the Universe.

The observable horizon – the edge of the known Universe – is about 14,000,000,000 light-years away.

| 100,000,000 | 9,000,000,000 | 10,000,000,000 | 11,000,000,000 | 12,000,000,000 | 13,000,000,000 | 14,000,000,000 | 15,000,000,000 |

The Solar System is located in the Orion Arm of the Milky Way.

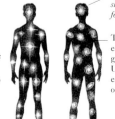

Plenty to go around

Nobody knows for sure, but there are an estimated 100,000,000,000 stars in the Milky Way, and about the same number of galaxies in the Universe. That is enough for you and every other person on Earth to stake a claim for 18 of each.

There are an estimated 18 stars in the Milky Way for each person on Earth.

I'll take eight spiral, six elliptical, and four irregular, please.

There are an estimated 18 galaxies in the Universe for each person on Earth.

WATER

WE LIVE IN A WET, wet world. Seen from space, some views of Earth show almost no land at all. Oceans cover more than two-thirds of our planet's surface. The largest ocean, the Pacific, covers nearly one-third of the globe and holds about half its water. In fact, 98 percent of all our world's water is in the sea. Most of the rest is locked up in the two great polar icecaps. Lakes hold just one five-thousandth of our world's water, rivers and streams even less. Clouds hold the least water of all – though you wouldn't think so if you were caught in a tropical rain storm without an umbrella!

Each side of this pool would be about as long as the distance between New York and Perth, Australia.

The Moon is 2,161 miles (3,477 km) wide. It would take at least 25 Moons to cover the surface of all the oceans.

Pooled together

Spread out with straight edges, like a swimming pool, all the world's oceans would form a square with sides about 11,806 miles (19,000 km) long – more than five times the diameter of the Moon.

All tanked up

The vast Pacific Ocean contains more water than all the world's other seas and oceans put together. A square tank big enough to hold it would have sides 551 miles (886 km) long.

Lake Nyasa, Malawi/Mozambique: 2,316 ft (706 m)

Lake Baikal: 5,315 ft (1,620 m)

North Sea: 2,165 ft (660 m)

Lake Superior, US/Canada: 30 ft (9 m)

The Pacific Ocean holds 167,000,000 cubic miles (696,000,000 cubic km) of water.

Plumbing the depths

The world's deepest freshwater lake, Russia's Lake Baikal, reaches 5,315 ft (1,620 m) at its deepest point. The mud at the bottom of the lake is even deeper. Compared with the deepest points in the world's oceans and seas, however, Lake Baikal is shallow. The deepest place in the world is the Marianas Trench in the Pacific Ocean.

Mt. Everest, in the Himalayas, is the world's tallest mountain at 29,028 ft (8,848 m). It would take more than 100 Mt. Everests stacked on top of one another to reach the surface of this tank.

Gulf of Mexico: 12,425 ft (3,787 m)

South China Sea: 16,456 ft (5,016 m)

Caribbean Sea: 22,788 ft (6,946 m)

Indian Ocean: 24,460 ft (7,455 m)

The Statue of Liberty, in New York, is 305 ft (93 m) high. If all the world's ice melted, poor Liberty would drown – only her torch would show above the waves.

About 71 percent of the Earth's surface is water.

Present sea level

Atlantic Ocean: 30,246 ft (9,219 m)

The Empire State Building is 1,250 ft (381 m) high. It would take a stack of 29 Empire State Buildings to reach the surface of the sea from the bottom of the Marianas Trench.

Marianas Trench, Pacific Ocean: 35,820 ft (10,918 m)

Rising damp

Only a small proportion of our world's water is locked up in glaciers and the two polar icecaps, but if they all melted, sea levels would rise dramatically – by about 262 ft (80 m).

Land and sea

The oceans dominate the Earth's surface, just 29 percent of which is above sea level. Global warming would reduce the land area still further because melting ice would raise sea levels, flooding low-lying coastal land.

Only 29 percent of the Earth's surface is land.

On the crest of a wave

Ordinary sea waves are whipped up by the wind. The highest wave ever recorded was in the Pacific Ocean in 1933 and measured 112 ft (34 m) from trough to crest.

Sea tops lake stakes

The landlocked Caspian Sea is the world's largest lake by area, but it is slightly salty. The largest freshwater lake by area is Lake Superior, one of the Great Lakes, in North America.

Lake Baikal: 12,160 sq miles (31,494 sq km)

Aral Sea, Kazakhstan/Uzbekistan: 15,444 sq miles (40,000 sq km)

Lake Victoria, East Africa: 24,301 sq miles (62,940 sq km)

Lake Superior, US/Canada: 31,761 sq miles (82,260 sq km)

Caspian Sea, Europe/Asia: 146,101 sq miles (378,400 sq km)

The 77,000,000 cubic miles (323,000,000 cubic km) of the Atlantic Ocean would fill a square tank with 426-mile (686-km) sides.

A square tank holding the 68,000,000 cubic miles (284,000,000 cubic km) of the Indian Ocean would need to have sides 408 miles (657 km) long.

Tall fallers

The world's highest waterfall, Angel Falls, in Venezuela, is 3,212 ft (979 m) tall. The longest drop on the falls is a more modest 2,648 ft (807 m), but that is still more than twice the height of the Eiffel Tower.

Angel Falls, Venezuela: 3,212 ft (979 m)

Utigård, Norway: 2,625 ft (800 m)

Yosemite Falls, California: 2,425 ft (739 m)

Eiffel Tower: 1,052 ft (321 m)

Sutherland Falls, New Zealand: 1,903 ft (580 m)

Victoria Falls, Zambia/Zimbabwe: 354 ft (108 m)

Niagara Falls (American): 167 ft (51 m)

Lake Superior: 2,921 cubic miles (12,174 cubic km)

Lake Baikal: 5,519 cubic miles (22,995 cubic km)

Seawater: 97.2 percent

Ice: 2.15 percent

All other water: 0.65 percent

Owen Falls: 49 cubic miles (205 cubic km)

Almost all at sea

Seawater and ice make up 99.35 percent of all the Earth's water. Almost all of the rest is groundwater stored in porous rocks. Lakes, rivers, and water in the atmosphere make up only 0.0015 percent of the Earth's water – a quarter of a teaspoonful for each bathful of seawater.

High Aswan, Egypt: 40 cubic miles (168 cubic km)

Puddles by comparison

Compared with natural lakes, even the largest artificial reservoirs seem like puny efforts. Lake Baikal, the world's largest freshwater lake by volume, would fill Uganda's Owen Falls, the world's biggest artificial reservoir, 112 times.

Guri, Venezuela: 33 cubic miles (136 cubic km)

Zeya, Russia: 16 cubic miles (68 cubic km)

Daily output of water from the Amazon

Water in Lake Baikal

Amazing Amazon

The Amazon River, in Brazil, discharges about 2.5 cubic miles (10.5 cubic km) of water a minute into the Atlantic Ocean. That is enough for everyone in the world to have a bath every 40 minutes, allowing 21 gallons (80 liters) per bath. If the Amazon drained Lake Baikal, the lake would be two-thirds empty in just one day.

Hidden depths

Although it appears quite small in area, Lake Baikal is extremely deep and contains more water than any other freshwater lake. Lake Superior, the biggest freshwater lake by area, looks bigger, but holds a much smaller volume of water.

Shock waves

Earthquakes and volcanoes can cause especially big waves called tsunamis. The tallest recorded tsunami reached the remarkable height of 278 ft (85 m).

Ahoy there! I'm on this boat, but I'm so small you can hardly see me.

MOUNTAINS

THE WORLD'S HIGHEST natural features, the great mountains, dwarf even the biggest buildings. The tallest mountain of all is Mt. Everest, in the Himalayas. The air at the top of Everest is three times as thin as the air at sea level. What with the numbing cold, thin air, and icy rock faces, it takes even the best prepared and most experienced of climbers weeks to reach the top of Everest.

On top of the world

The 35 highest mountains in the world are all in the Himalayan and Karakoram ranges, between China and the Indian subcontinent. The top five are Everest, K2, Kanchenjunga, Lhotse I, and Makalu I. Everest is 27 times as high as the Eiffel Tower. An office building the same height would have at least 2,000 floors.

Everest:
29,028 ft
(8,848 m)

K2:
28,250 ft
(8,611 m)

Kanchenjunga:
28,208 ft
(8,597 m)

Lhotse I:
27,923 ft
(8,511 m)

Makalu I:
27,824 ft
(8,481 m)

At 29,028 ft (8,848 m), Mt. Everest towers over the tallest volcanoes. It is half as high again as Mt. Kilimanjaro, more than twice as high as Mt. Fuji, and nearly seven times as high as Mt. Vesuvius.

Mt. Kilimanjaro, in Tanzania, rises to 19,344 ft (5,896 m), making it the highest point in Africa.

Mt. Fuji is the highest peak in Japan at 12,388 ft (3,776 m).

Mt. Vesuvius, in Italy, is 4,190 ft (1,277 m) high.

Mt. Aconcagua, in the Andes, is the highest mountain in the Americas at 22,834 ft (6,960 m).

Everest dwarfs volcanoes

Even the highest volcanoes, such as Mt. Kilimanjaro, fall short of Mt. Everest. Size is relative, however – although Kilimanjaro is 9,685 ft (2,952 m) shorter than Everest, Kilimanjaro is still 40 times higher than the Great Pyramid, in Egypt.

Sunken volcano

Mauna Kea   Mt. Everest

Mauna Kea is a volcano in Hawaii. Its base is on the seabed. Measured from there, rather than from sea level, it is 4,446 ft (1,355 m) taller than Mt. Everest.

Mt. Elbrus, Russia: 18,510 ft (5,642 m)

Mt. Cook is New Zealand's highest peak at 12,316 ft (3,754 m).

Helen blows her top

Mt. St. Helen's, a volcano in Washington state, erupted in 1980, throwing huge clouds of ash high into the sky. The ash devastated about 210 sq miles (550 sq km), an area the size of more than 2,100 tennis courts. Before the eruption the volcano was some 9,678 ft (2,950 m) high; afterward it was about 1,310 ft (400 m) shorter.

Mt. St. Helen's: 8,366 ft (2,550 m)

Conifer treeline: 8,202 ft (2,500 m)

Broadleaf treeline: 3,937 ft (1,200 m)

29,528 ft (9,000 m)

26,247 ft (8,000 m)

22,966 ft (7,000 m)

19,685 ft (6,000 m)

16,404 ft (5,000 m)

13,123 ft (4,000 m)

9,843 ft (3,000 m)

6,562 ft (2,000 m)

3,281 ft (1,000 m)

0

Mt. Everest:
29,028 ft
(8,848 m)

Martian mammoth

The highest volcano in the Solar System
is Olympus Mons, on Mars. It is three
times higher than Mt. Everest,
and nine times higher than
Mt. Olympus, in Greece.
It is thought to be
extinct.

Mt. Everest

Olympus Mons is
about 86,614 ft
(26,400 m) high.

Yaks can live at heights of
more than 19,685 ft (6,000 m).

Edmund Hillary and Sherpa
Tenzing, the first people to
climb Mt. Everest, pitched
their base camp at 18,000 ft
(5,486 m).

Mt. McKinley, in the
Alaska Range, is the
highest mountain in
the US at 20,320 ft
(6,194 m)

Vinson Massif, Antarctica:
16,864 ft (5,140 m)

The air at altitude

The higher you climb, the colder the air
becomes – the temperature falls about 11°F
(6°C) every 3,281 ft (1,000 m). Climbers
wear special clothing to keep warm. The air
also becomes thinner. This means there is
less oxygen in each lungful of air. Climbers
either allow time for their bodies to adapt, or
take extra oxygen supplies.

*I'm level with Hillary
and Tenzing's base
camp on Everest. Even
here the air is twice as
thin as at sea level, and
it's hard to breathe.*

The Matterhorn, in
the European Alps,
is 14,691 ft (4,478 m)
above sea level.

Mont Blanc, in the
European Alps:
15,770 ft (4,807 m)

Toverkop,
in South
Africa, rises
to 7,644 ft
(2,330 m).

Tall buildings (see pages 48-49), at the same scale as the mountains. Even
Toverkop is nearly four times as tall as the world's tallest artificial structure,
the 2,063-ft (629-m) KTHI-TV tower, in North Dakota.

29,528 ft
(9,000 m)

26,247 ft
(8,000 m)

22,966 ft
(7,000 m)

19,685 ft
(6,000 m)

16,404 ft
(5,000 m)

13,123 ft
(4,000 m)

9,843 ft
(3,000 m)

6,562 ft
(2,000 m)

3,281 ft
(1,000 m)

0

GREAT LENGTHS

"IT'S HUGE! COLOSSAL! AMAZING!" How do you describe something so large it makes you dizzy to look at it? Countless words have been written about the world's great wonders, but nothing can prepare you for the awe-inspiring experience of seeing them, or comprehending their vastness, for the first time. No structures built by humans can match nature's greatest marvels, but some of them are still pretty impressive. For instance, you could drive around the US at top speed 24 hours a day for four years – and still not cover every stretch of road.

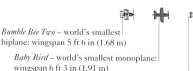

Bumble Bee Two – world's smallest biplane: wingspan 5 ft 6 in (1.68 m)

Baby Bird – world's smallest monoplane: wingspan 6 ft 3 in (1.91 m)

Albatross: wingspan 12 ft (3.7 m)

Marabou stork: wingspan 13 ft (4 m)

Silver Bullet – world's smallest jet plane: wingspan 17 ft (5.2 m)

Winged wonders of the world

A biplane (double-winged plane) called *Bumble Bee Two*, built in the 1980s by Robert H. Starr of Arizona, had a wingspan no wider than the outstretched arms of its pilot. At the other extreme, you could park 50 cars side by side on the wings of *Spruce Goose*, a flying-boat built in the US in the 1940s by Howard Hughes, an eccentric billionaire. *Spruce Goose* barely made it into the air on its maiden flight and covered a distance less than 10 times its own wingspan. It has not flown since and is now on display at a museum (a very big one).

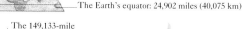

US – road network: 3,990,056 miles (6,420,000 km)

India – road network: 1,280,298 miles (2,060,000 km)

Brazil – road network: 1,230,557 miles (1,980,000 km)

US – rail network: 149,133 miles (240,000 km)

Russia – rail network: 95,711 miles (154,000 km)

China – waterways: 86,124 miles (138,600 km)

Russia – waterways: 62,771 miles (101,000 km)

Canada – rail network: 45,346 miles (72,963 km)

Brazil – waterways: 31,069 miles (50,000 km)

On the road

The webs of roads and railroads that crisscross the globe are perhaps the biggest objects ever built. The US road network tops the league – you could drive around the US at 100 mph (161 kph) nonstop for four years and still not cover every stretch of road. You would pass plenty of other cars, though: there are more than 141 million cars in the US – one for every 144 ft (44 m) of road.

All around the world – and the Sun

The rail network of the US could go around the Earth's equator almost six times – yet it is tiny compared with the US road network. That is so vast that it could go all the way around the Sun's equator – then part of the way around again (although you would need heatproof tires and a strong nerve to brave the melting pavement).

The Earth's equator: 24,902 miles (40,075 km)

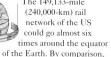

The 149,133-mile (240,000-km) rail network of the US could go almost six times around the equator of the Earth. By comparison, the world's shortest rail network goes almost nowhere – Vatican City, the world's smallest state, has just 2,789 ft (850 m) of track.

US – rail network: 149,133 miles (240,000 km)

The Earth's equator: 24,902 miles (40,075 km)

Martian metro

The world's largest metropolitan railroad has enough track to cover the length of the base of the biggest mountain in the Solar System.

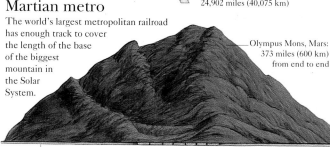

Olympus Mons, Mars: 373 miles (600 km) from end to end

Metropolitan railroad system, Tokyo, Japan: 391 miles (629 km)

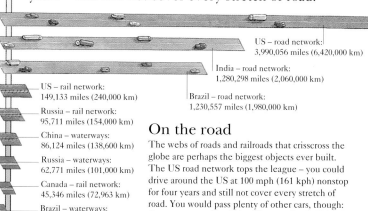

The Grand Canyon averages 1 mile (1.6 km) deep and is 277 miles (446 km) long. Eroding a layer of rock the thickness of a credit card every five years, it took the Colorado River about 10 million years to excavate the gorge – an astonishingly short time in geological terms.

Sliding slowly toward the sea, the Lambert-Fischer Glacier, in Antarctica, is 320 miles (515 km) long.

The Mammoth Cave system, the world's most extensive, is 352 miles (567 km) long and riddles Kentucky with holes!

Naturally very long

The longest of the Earth's natural features – the great rivers and mountain ranges – are truly colossal. The longest of all stretches almost from pole to pole, but is entirely hidden from sight – it is the Mid-Atlantic Ridge, a huge underwater mountain range running the full length of the Atlantic Ocean.

Made of coral and home to a huge variety of fish and other marine animals, the Great Barrier Reef stretches 1,260 miles (2,028 km) along the coast of Queensland, Australia.

The Himalayas, Karakorams, and Hindu Kush together form an unbroken mountain range that is 2,400 miles (3,862 km) long.

The Mekong River winds 2,703 miles (4,350 km) through China, Laos, Thailand, Cambodia, and Vietnam before flowing into the South China Sea.

The Chiang Jiang River, in China, is 3,915 miles (6,300 km) long and carries half the country's riverboat traffic.

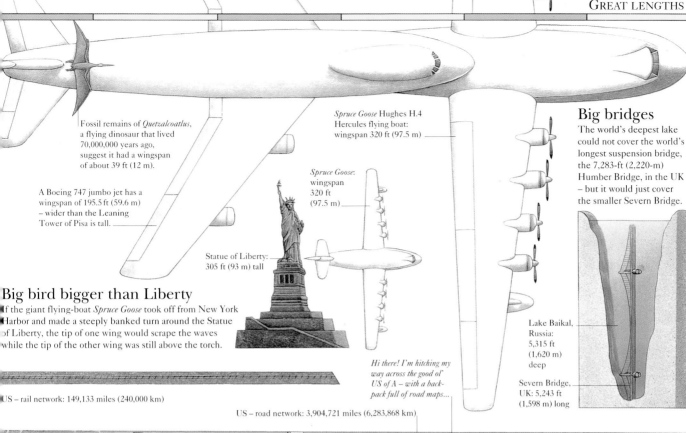

Fossil remains of *Quetzalcoatlus*, a flying dinosaur that lived 70,000,000 years ago, suggest it had a wingspan of about 39 ft (12 m).

A Boeing 747 jumbo jet has a wingspan of 195.5 ft (59.6 m) – wider than the Leaning Tower of Pisa is tall.

Spruce Goose Hughes H.4 Hercules flying boat: wingspan 320 ft (97.5 m)

Spruce Goose: wingspan 320 ft (97.5 m)

Statue of Liberty: 305 ft (93 m) tall

Big bridges

The world's deepest lake could not cover the world's longest suspension bridge, the 7,283-ft (2,220-m) Humber Bridge, in the UK – but it would just cover the smaller Severn Bridge.

Lake Baikal, Russia: 5,315 ft (1,620 m) deep

Severn Bridge, UK: 5,243 ft (1,598 m) long

Big bird bigger than Liberty

If the giant flying-boat *Spruce Goose* took off from New York Harbor and made a steeply banked turn around the Statue of Liberty, the tip of one wing would scrape the waves while the tip of the other wing was still above the torch.

Hi there! I'm hitching my way across the good ol' US of A – with a back-pack full of road maps...

US – rail network: 149,133 miles (240,000 km)

US – road network: 3,904,721 miles (6,283,868 km)

Sun's equator: 2,717,952 miles (4,374,000 km)

Linking the world

Laying telephone cables and oil pipelines is easier and cheaper than digging road and rail tunnels, which therefore tend to be much shorter.

First transatlantic telephone cable: 1,950 miles (3,138 km)

World's longest oil pipeline – Alberta, Canada, to New York: 1,775 miles (2,856 km)

London to Paris: 213 miles (342 km)

World's longest tunnel – water supply tunnel from New York City to Delaware: 105 miles (169 km)
World's longest railroad tunnel – Seikan, Japan: 33.5 miles (53.9 km)
English Channel railroad tunnel from the UK to France: 31 miles (50 km)
Metropolitan railroad tunnel, Moscow, Russia (Kalushskaya line): 23.5 miles (37.9 km)
World's longest road tunnel, St. Gotthard, Switzerland: 10 miles (16.3 km)

Entire coastline of New Zealand: 8,161 miles (13,134 km)

Cable across the sea

The longest telecommunications cable in the world runs across the bottom of the Pacific Ocean and links New Zealand and Australia to Canada. It is longer than New Zealand's coastline.

ANZCAN telecommunications cable: 9,415 miles (15,151 km)

Berlin

New York

At 4,007 miles (6,448 km), the Amazon River is longer than the distance from New York to Berlin – 3,968 miles (6,385 km).

At 4,500 miles (7,242 km), the Andes mountain range is longer than the distance from London to Bombay – 4,468 miles (7,190 km).

London

Bombay

At 4,145 miles (6,670 km), the Nile River, in Africa, is the longest in the world.

The Andes mountain range runs like a 4,500-mile (7,242-km) spine down the back of South America.

The Mid-Atlantic Ridge is a 7,022-mile (11,300-km) long mountain range under the sea.

South American wonders

Two of the world's longest natural features are found in South America. The Amazon River is longer than the distance from New York to Berlin, Germany, while the Andes mountain range is longer than the distance from London to Bombay, India.

St. Gotthard road tunnel: 53,543 ft (16,320 m)

Mountain marvel

The St. Gotthard road tunnel in the Swiss Alps is the longest in the world. It is almost twice as long as the height of the world's tallest mountain, Mt. Everest.

Mt. Everest: 29,028 ft (8,848 m)

3,728 miles (6,000 km) 4,350 miles (7,000 km) 4,971 miles (8,000 km) 5,592 miles (9,000 km) 6,214 miles (10,000 km)

WEATHER

WEATHER AFFECTS ALL of our lives, but to a greater or lesser degree depending on where we live. Some parts of the world are safe and fertile places, with comfortable amounts of sunshine, rain, and snow. Others are hot, inhospitable deserts, or frozen Arctic wastes. Then there are the hot and humid tropics – highly fertile lands, but in an area frequently ravaged by mighty storms and floods.

Hurricane force

In summer, islands and coastal countries in the tropics are sometimes hit by severe storms, known as hurricanes in the Gulf of Mexico and Caribbean, cyclones in the Indian Ocean, and typhoons in the north-western Pacific. They can last for 10 days or more, with winds of 100 mph (161 kph). Remarkably, the center, or eye, of a tropical storm is calm.

Typhoons covering an area larger than that of Bangladesh – 55,600 sq miles (143,998 sq km) – frequently sweep across this country, causing widespread flooding and destruction.

When Hurricane Camille hit the coast of Mississippi and Alabama in 1969, gusts of 200 mph (322 kph) were recorded – faster than the fastest motorcycle.

Twisting tornadoes

A tornado, or twister, is a rapidly spinning column of air that whirls dust and debris high into the sky and can destroy buildings. Tornadoes at sea are called waterspouts – although short-lived, they can whisk a column of water up to cloud level.

A tornado whirling at 280 mph (450 kph) – faster than Donald Campbell's record-breaking 1964 *Bluebird* speedboat, and nearly as fast as a dragster – struck Wichita Falls, in Texas, in 1958.

The Empire State Building is 1,250 ft (381 m) high. A waterspout four times as high, at 5,014 ft (1,528 m), was seen off Australia in 1898.

Bluebird speedboat: 277 mph (445 kph)

Dragster: 309 mph (497 kph)

Continental extremes

A comparison of the greatest extremes of temperature – the hottest and coldest on record for each continent – shows that Oceania has the smallest range and Asia the greatest.

MAXIMUM TEMPERATURE

Oceania: 127°F (53°C)

South America: 120°F (49°C)

Africa: 136°F (58°C)

Antarctica: 57°F (14°C)

Europe: 122°F (50°C)

North America: 135°F (57°C)

Asia: 129°F (54°C)

MINIMUM TEMPERATURE

Oceania: –8°F (–22°C)

South America: –27°F (–33°C)

Africa: –11°F (–24°C)

Antarctica: –128°F (–89°C)

Europe: –67°F (–55°C)

North America: –81°F (–63°C)

Asia: –90°F (–68°C)

The wind and the water

The Beaufort scale of wind speeds is used worldwide in weather reports and forecasts compiled for ships and boats at sea. It was invented in 1805 by British Admiral Sir Francis Beaufort. The scale ranges from Force 0, representing a calm sea, through Force 8, representing a gale, to Force 12 and above, signifying hurricane-strength winds.

0 – calm: 0-1 mph (0-2 kph)
1 – light air: 1-3 mph (2-5 kph)
2 – light breeze: 4-7 mph (6-11 kph)
3 – gentle breeze: 8-12 mph (12-19 kph)
4 – moderate breeze: 12-18 mph (20-29 kph)
5 – fresh breeze: 19-24 mph (30-38 kph)
6 – strong breeze: 24-31 mph (39-50 kph)
7 – high wind: 32-38 mph (51-61 kph)
8 – gale: 38-46 mph (62-74 kph)

Fire and ice

Between the fiery surface of the Sun and the absolute cold of space, there is only a narrow band of temperatures at which life is possible. Even within this narrow band there are huge variations, however – from the searing heat of some deserts to icy polar wastes.

Cloncurry, Australia, has recorded temperatures as high as 127°F (52.8°C).

Over the period 1960-66, an average temperature of 94°F (34.4°C) was recorded for Dallol, in Ethiopia – the hottest on Earth.

Water freezes at 32°F (0°C) at sea level.

A comfortable room temperature is considered to be 68°F (20°C).

The highest temperature ever recorded in the shade – 136°F (57.8°C), at al'Aziziyah, in the Libyan desert, in September 1922 – was hot enough to fry an egg.

The top summer temperature in Rome, Italy, is a hot but tolerable 104°F (40°C).

The surface of the Sun is a scorching 9,626°F (5,330°C).

At sea level, water boils at 212°F (100°C).

The temperature at the bottom of the world's deepest mines reaches 163°F (73°C).

That's much better!

194°F (90°C)   158°F (70°C)   122°F (50°C)   86°F (30°C)   50°F (10°C)

Clouds in the sky

The lowest clouds, stratus, form below 1,509 ft (460 m) – not much higher than the world's tallest office building, the 1,482-ft (452-m) high Petronas Towers, in Kuala Lumpur, Malaysia. The highest clouds, cirrus, can be seen at 44,948 ft (13,700 m) – nearly 16,404 ft (5,000 m) higher than the world's highest mountain.

I'm in a glider at 45,932 ft (14,000 m), almost its peak altitude, and I'm only just above the highest clouds.

Cirrus

Cirrostratus

Cumulonimbus

Cirrocumulus

Mt. Everest:
29,028 ft
(8,848 m)

Altocumulus

Altostratus

Cumulonimbus

Nimbostratus

Stratocumulus

Cumulus

Stratus

Fog

45,932 ft (14,000 m)

42,651 ft (13,000 m)

39,370 ft (12,000 m)

36,089 ft (11,000 m)

32,808 ft (10,000 m)

29,528 ft (9,000 m)

26,247 ft (8,000 m)

22,966 ft (7,000 m)

19,685 ft (6,000 m)

16,404 ft (5,000 m)

13,123 ft (4,000 m)

9,843 ft (3,000 m)

6,562 ft (2,000 m)

3,281 ft (1,000 m)

0

Lightning strikes

The Earth is struck by lightning 100 times a second. High-speed photography shows that each strike consists of a lead stroke and a return stroke. The lead stroke travels at 99-994 miles (160-1,600 km) per second and forks as it opens a channel from the clouds to the ground. The much brighter return stroke flashes up this channel at about 86,994 miles (140,000 km) per second, or nearly half the speed of light.

Lightning can extend up to 20 miles (32 km). A space shuttle takes only 100 seconds to travel this high from liftoff, but the return stroke of a lightning bolt is more than 400,000 times as fast.

A typical lightning bolt is about 2,625 ft (800 m) long – almost three times the height of the Eiffel Tower, which is 1,052 ft (321 m).

Leaning Tower of Pisa: 180 ft (55 m)

In the 12 months from February 19, 1971, to February 18, 1972, 102 ft (31 m) of snow fell on Mt. Rainier, Washington.

Tamarac, California: 37 ft 5 in (11.4 m) of snow fell during March 1911

New York receives an average of 2 ft 5 in (74 cm) of snow every year.

Tenpin hailstones

On September 3, 1970, hailstones up to 1 lb 11 oz (760 g) in weight and up to 8 in (20 cm) in diameter – as big as tenpin bowling balls – fell at Coffeyville, Kansas.

Rain around the world

Annual rainfall varies greatly worldwide. Aswan, in Egypt, has a measly 0.02 in (0.5 mm). However, Bonaventura, in Colombia, has a drenching 22 ft (6.7 m) – enough to cover almost four adults standing on each other's shoulders. Meanwhile, at Mt. Waialeale, in Hawaii, it rains up to 350 days every year.

Snowed under

There are records of nearly 6.5 ft (2 m) of snow falling in one day – enough to bury a standing adult. Single snowstorms have resulted in falls of almost 16 ft (5 m) – enough to cover three adults standing on each other's shoulders. In 12 months, enough snow falls on the world's snowiest place, Mt. Rainier, in Washington state, to bury more than half of the Leaning Tower of Pisa.

Cilaos, La Réunion, Indian Ocean, March 15-16, 1952 – highest ever rainfall in 24 hours: 6 ft 2 in (1.87 m)

Madrid, Spain: average annual rainfall 16.5 in (42 cm)

Cherrapunji, Assam, India, August 1, 1860-July 31, 1861 – highest annual total rainfall: 87 ft (26.5 m)

9 – strong gale: 47-53 mph (75-86 kph)
10 – whole gale: 54-63 mph (87-101 kph)
11 – storm: 63-71 mph (102-115 kph)

12 – hurricane: 72-82 mph (116-132 kph)
13 – hurricane: 83-93 mph (133-149 kph)
14 – hurricane: 93-103 mph (150-166 kph)

9

10

11

12

13

14

15

16

17

15-17: hurricanes of 103-135 mph (166-218 kph)... rarely encountered, but extremely destructive

Norilsk, Russia, is the coldest inhabited place in the world, with an average temperature of 12.4°F (–10.9°C).

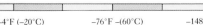

At an average –72°F (–57.8°C), Polus Nedostupnosti, in Antarctica, is the coldest place on Earth.

The coldest temperature ever recorded on the surface of the Earth was –128.6°F (–89.2°C), at Vostok, Antarctica, in 1983.

Temperatures in outer space plunge to within 4°F (3°C) of the coldest temperature possible, known as absolute zero: –459.69°F (–273.16°C).

The lowest temperature ever recorded in the upper atmosphere was –225°F (–143°C), 50 miles (80 km) above Kronogard, Sweden, in 1963.

–4°F (–20°C)   –76°F (–60°C)   –148°F (–100°C)   –220°F (–140°C)   –292°F (–180°C)   –364°F (–220°C)   –436°F (–260°C)

DISASTERS

"STOP THE PRESSES – HUNDREDS DIE in earthquake!" "Famine tragedy – thousands starve." Newspaper headlines and television news flashes like these elicit mixed emotions: shock at first, sympathy as we watch rescue workers and helpers – even excitement when we read about lucky escapes. We also feel relief that we are not among the victims, especially when the disaster happens close to home. It is easy to think, "It could have been me." Disasters on the other side of the world have much less impact on us, even when they are far more catastrophic.

Worldwide, modern tankers safely carry 60 bathtubfuls of crude oil for every teaspoonful accidentally spilled.

Some 92,460,506 gallons (350,000,000 liters) of crude oil spilled into the Carribean when the tankers *Atlantic Empress* and *Aegean Captain* collided off Trinidad & Tobago in 1979.

In 1978 the tanker *Amoco Cadiz* spilled 70,798,330 gallons (268,000,000 liters) of crude oil into the sea off the coast of France.

Oiling the waters

The largest oil tankers – supertankers – can carry as much as 172,000,000 gallons (650,000,000 liters) of crude oil at a time. That is about 1 gallon (4 liters) for every car in the US, so a major spill can spread over a vast area of the sea and pollute a huge length of coastline. Nothing can protect the oceans against deliberate releases of oil such as the one by Iraq during the Gulf War, however.

In 1991 Iraq deliberately discharged 449,093,880 gallons (1,700,000,000 liters) of crude oil into the Persian Gulf.

When the *Torrey Canyon* ran aground off the coast of Great Britain in 1967, it spilled 36,720,029 gallons (139,000,000 liters) of crude oil into the sea.

In 1989 the *Exxon Valdez* spilled 10,831,087 gallons (41,000,000 liters) of crude oil into the sea off the coast of Alaska.

The explosive eruption of the volcanic island of Krakatoa, triggered a 120-ft (37-m) high tsunami, or giant ocean wave.

Ships left high and dry

The Aral Sea, in Kazakhstan and Uzbekistan, was once the world's fourth biggest lake. Until the 1960s, 13 cubic miles (56 cubic km) of water flowed into it each year. Since the 1960s, 97 percent of this water has been diverted for irrigation and industry. As a result, the Aral Sea is steadily drying up. An area the size of Lake Tanganyika, in Africa, has already been lost. The lake now covers about half its original area – and ships are left rusting away on dry land, with the lake nowhere in sight.

Aral Sea in 1964: about 25,292 sq miles (65,500 sq km)

Aral Sea in 1993: about 14,094 sq miles (36,500 sq km)

Krakatoa catastrophe

In 1883 a series of huge blasts blew apart the volcanic island of Krakatoa, in Indonesia, killing 36,000 people. Heard some 2,983 miles (4,800 km) away, the blasts ejected 5 cubic miles (21 cubic km) of dust into the air – more than 8,000 times the volume of the Great Pyramid.

Sea takes greatest toll

Most of the worst transportation disasters are at sea, but since long-distance travelers switched to flying, plane crashes have grabbed the headlines. This makes some people afraid to fly, when in fact it is one of the safest forms of travel.

Challenger space shuttle, US, 1986: 7 die in explosion shortly after takeoff

Hindenburg airship, New Jersey, 1937: 36 die in mooring explosion

Le Mans motor racing circuit, France, 1955: 82 die when car crashes and explodes

Subway, New York, 1918: 97 die in train crash

Air India 747, Irish Sea, 1985: 329 die in midair aircraft explosion

Japan Air Lines 747, Japan, 1985: 520 die in mountain plane crash

KLM & Pan Am 747s, Canary Islands, 1977: 583 die in airport runway collision

Railroad, Bihar, India, 1981: 800 die when train plunges off bridge

Titanic passenger liner, North Atlantic, 1912: 1,517 die in sinking of ship after it hits iceberg

Sultana steamboat, Mississippi, 1865: 1,547 die in riverboat explosion

The biggest killers

Disease and famine kill far more people than wars or natural disasters. The Black Death killed up to three-quarters of all people in Europe in the 14th century. Without modern drugs, a similar plague today could kill four billion people.

Rat fleas spread the plague when they bite people.

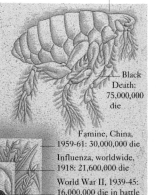

Malaria, spread by mosquito bites in the tropics: worldwide, 2,000,000 die each year

Korean War, 1950-53: 1,900,000 die in battle

Irish potato famine, 1846-51: 1,500,000 die

Bangladesh cyclone, 1970: 1,000,000 die

Black Death: 75,000,000 die

Famine, China, 1959-61: 30,000,000 die

Influenza, worldwide, 1918: 21,600,000 die

World War II, 1939-45: 16,000,000 die in battle

World War I, 1914-18: 8,500,000 die in battle

Salang Tunnel (road and rail), Afghanistan, 1982: 3,000 die in fuel tanker crash and explosion

Donna Paz ferry, Philippines, 1987: 3,000 die when oil tanker rams ferry

0   1,000 people   2,000 people   3,000 people

Explosive force

Some modern nuclear warheads are 1,250 times as powerful as the atomic bomb dropped on Hiroshima. But the Tunguska explosion was 1,500 times as powerful as the Hiroshima bomb, while the combined force of the four Krakatoa explosions was 10,000 times more powerful.

Hiroshima bomb
Equal to 22,400 tons (20,320 tonnes) of ordinary TNT explosive

Tunguska meteorite
Equal to 33.6 million tons (30.5 million tonnes) of TNT

Krakatoa volcano
Equal to 223 million tons (203 million tonnes) of TNT

Tunguska meteorite

Lava not the real killer

Not all volcanoes kill through sudden explosions or eruptions. In 1783, Laki volcano, in Iceland, spewed out lava – molten rock – for two months. The lava filled two valleys, but killed very few people directly. Most of the 10,000 deaths were caused by sulfurous fumes, and by starvation resulting from volcanic ash killing crops and animals.

The lava was 98 ft (30 m) deep – enough to bury a 66-ft (20-m) four-story town house.

Siberian shocker

One day in 1908 a blast filled the sky above Tunguska, in Siberia, a remote area of Russia. Heard 621 miles (1,000 km) away, it flattened trees over 1,931 sq miles (5,000 sq km), an area twice the size of Luxembourg, but no one was killed. Scientists believe a large meteorite exploded as it hit the upper atmosphere.

Only the very tip of the 1,815-ft (553-m) CN Tower, in Toronto, Canada, would clear the top of the cone.

Cone in a cornfield

The 1943 eruption of Parícutin, in Mexico, killed no one, but as the volcano grew, it engulfed a village and destroyed large areas of farmland. It appeared, almost without warning, in a cornfield.

Hiroshima

In 1945 an atomic bomb was dropped on the city of Hiroshima, in Japan. It killed about 140,000 people and almost totally destroyed the city.

Hiroshima atomic bomb

One day after the cone first appeared it was 33 ft (10 m) high.

Parícutin

Only one year after the cone appeared it was 1,476 ft (450 m) high. At the peak of its activity it was ejecting 2,690 tons (2,440 tonnes) of material a minute. In 1952 the cone was measured at 1,732 ft (528 m).

China's flood hazard

China's Yellow River regularly floods huge areas of farmland. Heavy rains in 1887 caused it to flood an area one-and-a-half times the size of Ireland. The areas devastated by some of the world's most famous city fires are tiny by comparison.

Great Fire of London, UK, 1666: 0.7 sq miles (1.9 sq km) destroyed

Chicago, Illinois, 1871: fire destroys 3.4 sq miles (8.9 sq km)

Yellow River, 1887: 48,266 sq miles (125,000 sq km) flooded

Area of Ireland: 32,377 sq miles (83,850 sq km)

Disaster areas

Diseases, such as the plague, can cause worldwide destruction, but most disasters are far less extensive. Those that have the most widespread effects are floods, which can drown small countries. Global warming, caused by atmospheric pollution trapping the Sun's heat, could cause worse floods than anything yet seen, as rising sea levels wash over coastal cities.

Bad vibrations

The Richter scale of earthquake size measures how much the ground moves, but is not a guide to the destruction caused – that depends much more on the structure of the rock and earth where the earthquake strikes, and on the construction of the local buildings.

San Francisco, 1906: 8.25 on the Richter scale, about 500 die

Wilhelm Gustloff refugee ship, Baltic Sea, 1945: 7,700 die when torpedoed ship sinks – death toll equal to almost 14 full jumbo jets

Tangshan, China, 1976: 7.8 on the Richter scale, 655,000 die

Kobe, Japan, 1995: 6.8 on the Richter scale, 4,800 die

Mt. St. Helen's, 1980: ash from volcano covers 212 sq miles (550 sq km)

Exxon Valdez oil spill, 1989: 500 sq miles (1,295 sq km)

San Francisco, 1906: fire caused by earthquake destroys 4.6 sq miles (12 sq km)

Bush fires, South Australia, 1983: 2,000 sq miles (5,180 sq km)

Mississippi River, 1927: floods cover 17,994 sq miles (46,600 sq km)

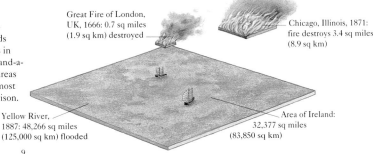

5,000 people   6,000 people   7,000 people   8,000 people

GREAT AND SMALL

COULD ANTS GROW big enough to eat people? Why are the largest animals living today found in the sea, and not on land? The simple answer to such fascinating questions is that animal size is governed by nature. We need not fear the jaws of giant insects because giant insects would soon suffocate – their simple breathing tubes could not supply them with enough air. Fierce competition for food stops the largest living land animals, elephants, from being bigger. When giant dinosaurs, which were far larger than elephants, roamed the Earth, they had no competitors. The biggest animals today, blue whales, feed freely on almost unlimited supplies of krill, a shrimplike creature. Whales' bodies are also adapted to the buoyancy of the sea. On land, they would be crushed by their own weight.

At up to 19 ft (5.8 m), a fully grown giraffe is so tall that its arteries have special valves to help pump blood up to its head. Without these valves, its heart would have to be as big as its whole body.

Twice as tall as all the rest

The giraffe is by far the tallest animal. It is up to twice as tall as the African elephant and more than three times as tall as the average man. Its long legs and long neck allow it to browse on treetop leaves beyond the reach of even an elephant's long trunk.

Adult bull African elephants grow more than 10 ft (3 m) tall.

Rearing on its hind legs, the grizzly bear of North America can be 10 ft (3 m) tall.

With its long legs and long neck, an ostrich can be 9 ft (2.7 m) t

Long gone Jurassic giant

The biggest dinosaurs were plant eaters. They were bigger than any living land animals because they had no competitors. One of the longest, measured from nose to tail tip, was *Diplodocus*, which lived on the North American continent some 145 million years ago. *Diplodocus* was nearly three times as long as the longest land animal living today, the reticulated python.

Found in Asia, and growing up to 35 ft (10.7 m) – almost half the length of a tennis court – the reticulated python is the longest snake in the world.

The Nile crocodile grows up to 16 ft (5 m) in length – more than 125 times as long as the world's smallest gecko.

Bull African elephants can be 16 ft (5 m) long – more than 23 ft (7 m) if you include their trunks and tails.

The Giant Indian rhinoceros grows up to 14 ft (4.3 m) long – about the length of a small car.

A dromedary camel can be 10 ft (3 m) long from the end of its nose to the base of its tail.

A tiger can be 9 ft (2.8 m) long – about six times as long as a domestic cat.

At 39 ft 4 in (12 m), the rare warm-water whale shark is about one-third as long as a blue whale. Luckily for us, it feeds on plankton and is completely harmless.

Gigantic jellyfish

In the buoyant, food-rich world of the sea, animals can grow to enormous sizes. The blue whale has the longest body, but if you include the tentacles, the Arctic giant jellyfish is the longest sea creature of all. Fanned out, its tentacles would form a circle covering an area bigger than 15 tennis courts.

Including their tentacles, giant deep-sea squid can be up to 57 ft (17.5 m) long.

The giant spider crab, found off Japan, has a body only about 10 in (25 cm) in diameter, but a leg span of up to 12 ft (3.7 m).

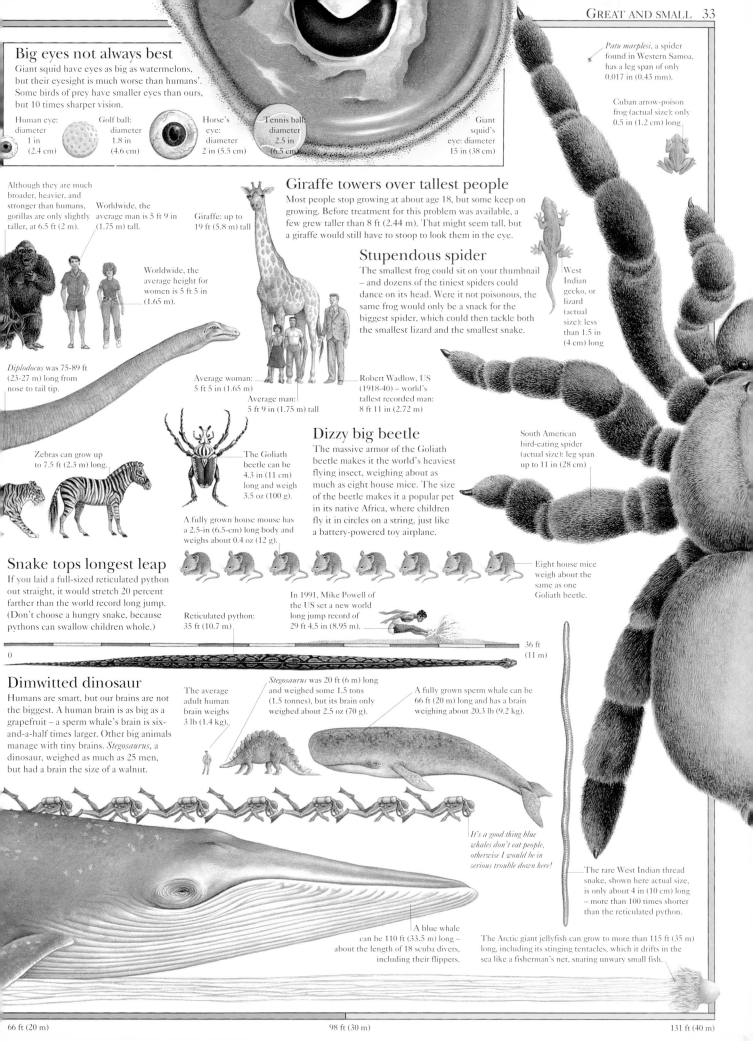

Big eyes not always best

Giant squid have eyes as big as watermelons, but their eyesight is much worse than humans'. Some birds of prey have smaller eyes than ours, but 10 times sharper vision.

Human eye: diameter 1 in (2.4 cm)

Golf ball: diameter 1.8 in (4.6 cm)

Horse's eye: diameter 2 in (5.5 cm)

Tennis ball: diameter 2.5 in (6.5 cm)

Giant squid's eye: diameter 15 in (38 cm)

Patu marplesi, a spider found in Western Samoa, has a leg span of only 0.017 in (0.43 mm).

Cuban arrow-poison frog (actual size): only 0.5 in (1.2 cm) long

Giraffe towers over tallest people

Most people stop growing at about age 18, but some keep on growing. Before treatment for this problem was available, a few grew taller than 8 ft (2.44 m). That might seem tall, but a giraffe would still have to stoop to look them in the eye.

Although they are much broader, heavier, and stronger than humans, gorillas are only slightly taller, at 6.5 ft (2 m).

Worldwide, the average man is 5 ft 9 in (1.75 m) tall.

Giraffe: up to 19 ft (5.8 m) tall

Worldwide, the average height for women is 5 ft 5 in (1.65 m).

Stupendous spider

The smallest frog could sit on your thumbnail – and dozens of the tiniest spiders could dance on its head. Were it not poisonous, the same frog would only be a snack for the biggest spider, which could then tackle both the smallest lizard and the smallest snake.

West Indian gecko, or lizard (actual size): less than 1.5 in (4 cm) long

Diplodocus was 75-89 ft (23-27 m) long from nose to tail tip.

Average woman: 5 ft 5 in (1.65 m)

Average man: 5 ft 9 in (1.75 m) tall

Robert Wadlow, US (1918-40) – world's tallest recorded man: 8 ft 11 in (2.72 m)

Dizzy big beetle

The massive armor of the Goliath beetle makes it the world's heaviest flying insect, weighing about as much as eight house mice. The size of the beetle makes it a popular pet in its native Africa, where children fly it in circles on a string, just like a battery-powered toy airplane.

South American bird-eating spider (actual size): leg span up to 11 in (28 cm)

Zebras can grow up to 7.5 ft (2.3 m) long.

The Goliath beetle can be 4.3 in (11 cm) long and weigh 3.5 oz (100 g).

A fully grown house mouse has a 2.5-in (6.5-cm) long body and weighs about 0.4 oz (12 g).

Eight house mice weigh about the same as one Goliath beetle.

Snake tops longest leap

If you laid a full-sized reticulated python out straight, it would stretch 20 percent farther than the world record long jump. (Don't choose a hungry snake, because pythons can swallow children whole.)

In 1991, Mike Powell of the US set a new world long jump record of 29 ft 4.5 in (8.95 m).

Reticulated python: 35 ft (10.7 m)

0

36 ft (11 m)

Dimwitted dinosaur

Humans are smart, but our brains are not the biggest. A human brain is as big as a grapefruit – a sperm whale's brain is six-and-a-half times larger. Other big animals manage with tiny brains. *Stegosaurus*, a dinosaur, weighed as much as 25 men, but had a brain the size of a walnut.

The average adult human brain weighs 3 lb (1.4 kg).

Stegosaurus was 20 ft (6 m) long and weighed some 1.5 tons (1.5 tonnes), but its brain only weighed about 2.5 oz (70 g).

A fully grown sperm whale can be 66 ft (20 m) long and has a brain weighing about 20.3 lb (9.2 kg).

It's a good thing blue whales don't eat people, otherwise I would be in serious trouble down here!

The rare West Indian thread snake, shown here actual size, is only about 4 in (10 cm) long – more than 100 times shorter than the reticulated python.

A blue whale can be 110 ft (33.5 m) long – about the length of 18 scuba divers, including their flippers.

The Arctic giant jellyfish can grow to more than 115 ft (35 m) long, including its stinging tentacles, which it drifts in the sea like a fisherman's net, snaring unwary small fish.

LIGHT AND HEAVY

SIZE AND WEIGHT do not always go hand in hand. A hummingbird and a golf ball are nearly the same size, but it takes as many as 28 hummingbirds to equal the weight of one golf ball. The heaviest metal, osmium, weighs more than 40 times as much as the lightest, lithium. The range of weights in both the human and natural worlds is enormous. The world's largest bell, the Tsar Kolokol bell, weighs almost as much as the Statue of Liberty, yet the statue is more than seven times as tall – while the heaviest mammal, the blue whale, can weigh an incredible 90,000,000 times more than the lightest, the pygmy shrew.

From heavy metal to lightweight lithium

The heaviest metal, and the heaviest element, is osmium. A 12-in (30-cm) cube of osmium would weigh about 1,345 lb (610 kg), or as much as 10 adults, each weighing 134 lb (61 kg). A 12-in (30-cm) cube of lithium, the lightest metal, would tip the scales at only 32 lb (14.4 kg) – not much heavier than the average two-year-old boy.

A 12-in (30-cm) cube of osmium would weigh as much as ten 134-lb (61-kg) adults.

The average two-year-old boy weighs 26 lb (11.8 kg).

A 12-in (30-cm) cube of lithium would weigh only 32 lb (14.4 kg).

Large weight of living wood

The largest living thing on Earth is the General Sherman giant sequoia tree, in Sequoia National Park, California. It weighs an estimated 2,756 tons (2,500 tonnes) – almost as much as a fuel-laden *Saturn V* rocket at liftoff.

At liftoff, a *Saturn V* rocket stood 364 ft (111 m) tall and weighed more than 3,263 tons (2,960 tonnes).

Almost a rocket a story

Built between 1929 and 1931, the rocket-shaped 102-story concrete and steel Empire State Building weighs about as much as 112 *Saturn V* rockets at liftoff.

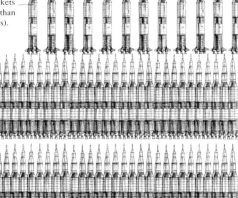

The Empire State Building weighs 365,000 tons (331,122 tonnes).

Altogether, 112 *Saturn V* rockets at liftoff would weigh more than 365,438 tons (331,520 tonnes).

Where did that rocket come from? Suddenly climbing this tree doesn't seem like such a good idea!

The General Sherman giant sequoia is nearly 276 ft (84 m) tall and weighs an estimated 2,756 tons (2,500 tonnes).

Lighter and heavier than air

All the hydrogen in *Graf Zeppelin II* weighed less than 20 tons (18 tonnes).

An adult bull African elephant weighs about 5.5 tons (5 tonnes).

Hydrogen is the lightest gas, radon the heaviest. *Graf Zeppelin II*, one of the two largest ever airships, held almost 7,062,940 cubic ft (200,000 cubic m) of hydrogen, weighing a little more than three bull African elephants. Filled with radon, it could not have flown – the gas would have weighed as much as 400 elephants.

Graf Zeppelin II was about 804 ft (245 m) long.

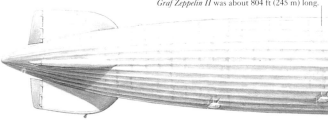

Had *Graf Zeppelin II* been filled with radon, the gas would have weighed more than 2,205 tons (2,000 tonnes) – as much as 400 bull African elephants.

A whale of a rocket

A *Saturn V* rocket at liftoff weighed about as much as 23 fully grown blue whales. Most of the weight was accounted for by three full fuel tanks and three sets of engines, which were fired and jettisoned in succession.

Adult blue whales weigh about 143 tons (130 tonnes) each – so 23 adult blue whales weigh about 3,296 tons (2,990 tonnes).

Saturn V rocket: more than 3,263 tons (2,960 tonnes)

Tower's iron tonnage

Modifications to the Eiffel Tower steadily increased its weight from the original 10,692 tons (9,700 tonnes) when it was completed in 1889. But in 1983 it was reduced to its present 9,653 tons (8,757 tonnes) – almost three times the weight of a *Saturn V* rocket at liftoff.

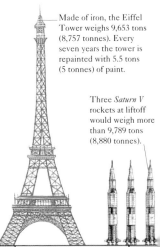

Made of iron, the Eiffel Tower weighs 9,653 tons (8,757 tonnes). Every seven years the tower is repainted with 5.5 tons (5 tonnes) of paint.

Three *Saturn V* rockets at liftoff would weigh more than 9,789 tons (8,880 tonnes).

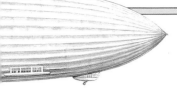

Twenty-eight bee hummingbirds

=

One 1.6-oz (45-g) golf ball

Small for their size...

A bee hummingbird, the world's smallest bird, weighs only about 0.06 oz (1.6 g), while a pygmy shrew, the world's smallest mammal, weighs only about 0.05 oz (1.5 g). Both are about the size of a golf ball, but one 1.6-oz (45-g) golf ball weighs as much as 28 bee hummingbirds or 30 pygmy shrews.

Thirty pygmy shrews

=

One 1.6-oz (45-g) golf ball

Mammoth mammals

Blue whales are the largest animals on Earth. Nobody has ever managed to weigh one intact, but they grow to an estimated 143 tons (130 tonnes) – about 26 times as heavy as a bull African elephant, the largest animal on land. In turn, a bull African elephant is about 26 times heavier than the average pig. Like pygmy shrews, blue whales are mammals – but they can be an incredible 90,000,000 times as heavy.

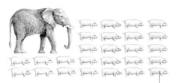

The average pig weighs 423 lb (192 kg). A bull African elephant weighs some 5.5 tons (5 tonnes) – about the same as 26 pigs.

One 143-ton (130-tonne) blue whale weighs about as much as 26 bull African elephants.

Jumbo flying bird

The ostrich is the biggest bird on Earth, but, although it can run fast, it is unable to fly. The heaviest bird that can fly is the great bustard, which can weigh as much as the average six-year-old boy – and more than 13,000 times as much as a bee hummingbird.

The average six-year-old boy weighs 46 lb (20.9 kg).

A fully grown great bustard can also weigh 46 lb (20.9 kg).

Lightweight Liberty

Excluding the pedestal, the Statue of Liberty is surprisingly light – only about one-and-a-half times the weight of a fully grown blue whale. It weighs much less than you might expect because, rather than being solid, it is a thin layer of copper over an iron framework.

The Statue of Liberty weighs only 225 tons (204 tonnes).

A fully grown blue whale weighs about 143 tons (130 tonnes).

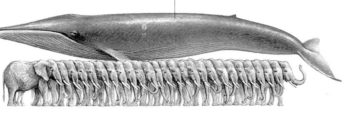

Worth its weight...

Throughout human history, gold has been coveted and valued for its beauty and rarity. Gold is also one of the heaviest of all metals. It is estimated that all the gold ever mined would weigh a total of about 165,347 tons (150,000 tonnes). That sounds like a lot, but in fact it would only make a solid block about the size of a tennis court.

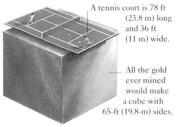

A tennis court is 78 ft (23.8 m) long and 36 ft (11 m) wide.

All the gold ever mined would make a cube with 65-ft (19.8-m) sides.

Big bronze bell

The world's largest bell is the Tsar Kolokol bell at the Kremlin, in Moscow, Russia. Cast from bronze in 1735, it cracked, and has never rung. Amazingly, it is almost as heavy as the much bigger Statue of Liberty.

Excluding the pedestal, the Statue of Liberty is 151 ft (46 m) tall and weighs 225 tons (204 tonnes).

The Tsar Kolokol bell is 20 ft (6.14 m) high and weighs 223 tons (201.9 tonnes).

Person drawn to scale

Solid as a rock

Made from more than 2,000,000 blocks of limestone, the Great Pyramid weighs almost 16 times as much as the Empire State Building – which, remarkably, weighs less than the 56-ft (17-m) deep chunk of earth that was excavated for its foundations.

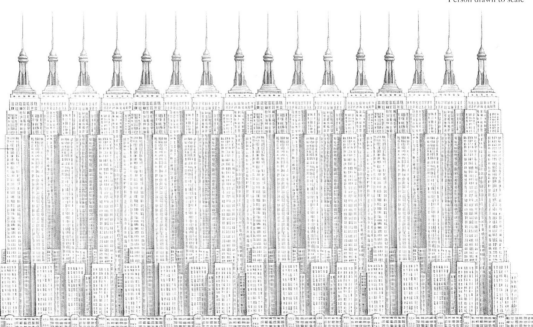

One Empire State Building weighs 365,000 tons (331,122 tonnes) – so 16 of them would weigh 5,839,985 tons (5,297,952 tonnes).

The Great Pyramid weighs an estimated 5,750,090 tons (5,216,400 tonnes).

ANIMAL SPEED

SOME ANIMALS ARE CAPABLE of great speed, which they use to chase prey or to escape from predators. Other animals live much more leisurely lives. From the proverbial slowness of the snail to the legendary swiftness of the cheetah – more than 2,000 times as fast – the range of speeds found in the animal world is astonishing. Recording them is not easy, however. Measuring how fast an animal can swim or fly is especially tricky, and it is difficult to tell a sudden spurt from an animal's normal top speed.

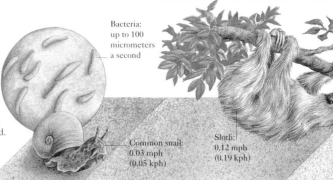

Micro movers
The speed of microscopic creatures is expressed in micrometers (millionths of a meter) a second.

Bacteria: up to 100 micrometers a second

Common snail: 0.03 mph (0.05 kph)

Sloth: 0.12 mph (0.19 kph)

Snail's pace
Even at its fastest, the common snail is 100 times slower than a child's normal walking speed.

FLYING THROUGH THE AIR

Birds were the world's fastest creatures until diving World War I aircraft began to exceed even the speed of a diving peregrine falcon, which can touch 217 mph (350 kph). With the aid of wind and gravity, even very small birds can manage 60 mph (97 kph).

Dragonfly: 18 mph (29 kph)

Darting by
Dragonflies are the fastest insects in the world, flying at up to 18 mph (29 kph) – maybe even faster.

As the crow flies
Crows and other common birds average speeds of 20-30 mph (32-48 kph).

Crow: 20-30 mph (32-48 kph)

Guano bat: 32 mph (51 kph)

Batmobility
Active only at night, the speedy guano bat uses sonar to stop it from flying into things in the dark.

CHAMPION RUNNERS

Some land animals, such as cheetahs, are sprinters, capable of sudden but short bursts of speed. Others, like elephants, are slower, but can maintain a steady pace for longer.

If cheetahs had to go to school every day, I bet they would be even slower than me!

Heavy going
Despite its great bulk, a charging African elephant can hit 25 mph (40 kph), easily outrunning a human athlete.

African elephant: 25 mph (40 kph)

First steps
A child's normal walking speed – except on the way to school – is just under 3 mph (5 kph).

Child walking: a little less than 3 mph (5 kph)

Fast track
Humans can run a long way at a steady pace, but can only sprint in short bursts. The men's world 100 m record is just under 10 seconds.

Cat: 30 mph (48 kph)

Female sprinter: 21 mph (34 kph)

Male sprinter: 22 mph (36 kph)

Rocketing ratcatchers
Cats can accelerate to 30 mph (48 kph) – which is bad luck for rats, with a top speed of less than 6 mph (10 kph).

SWIM KINGS RULE THE WAVES

The fastest fish and mammals in the sea are generally those with long bodies and powerful tails. Although they rarely exceed 10 times their own body length per second, and the endurance of many is limited, some species are awesome performers in the water.

Male swimmer: 5 mph (8 kph)

Dolphin: 30 mph (48 kph)

Gentoo penguin: 22 mph (35 kph)

In the swim
Dolphins can swim at 30 mph (48 kph), and maintain this speed over long distances.

Penguin power
The gentoo penguin of the Antarctic is thought to be the fastest swimming bird in the world.

At full stretch
Compared with many animals, human swimmers are slowpokes in the water, with 5 mph (8 kph) the apparent limit for a male Olympic freestyle swimmer.

Sea trout: 15 mph (24 kph)

Quick fish
Sea trout can swim five times as fast as a child can walk.

Tiger shark: 33 mph (53 kph)

Fast shark
Tiger sharks can swim six times faster than the fastest humans.

0 | 6 mph (10 kph) | 12 mph (20 kph) | 16 mph (25 kph) | 22 mph (35 kph) | 28 mph (45 kph) | 31 mph (50 kph)

Slow but sure

In the fable, the tortoise won the race against the hare. In real life, the tortoise is one of the slowest animals on land.

Slothful progress

Nonstop, it would take a sloth 24 years to stroll around the equator. As sloths sleep for up to 20 hours a day, however, the journey would actually take closer to 144 years.

SLOWPOKES OF THE ANIMAL WORLD

Some animals are genuine slowpokes, but others are handicapped by their tiny size. The top speed of about 3 mph (5 kph) of some cockroaches, for instance, is actually a scorching 50 body lengths a second. If a racehorse could do this, it would be able to run at about 304 mph (490 kph) – three times the top speed of a standard car.

A flurry of little legs

Large spiders in a hurry can scamper along at 1.1 mph (1.8 kph), but only for a few seconds.

Spider: 1.1 mph (1.8 kph)

Tortoise: 0.23 mph (0.37 kph)

Slow bird

The American woodcock is a real dawdler, flying just fast enough to stay in the air.

American woodcock: 5 mph (8 kph)

Harpy eagle: 37-50 mph (60-80 kph)

Swoop to kill

Birds of prey are at their fastest when diving. The fierce harpy eagle uses its speed to swoop down and pluck monkeys and sloths from the branches of trees.

Flight of fancy

Although higher speeds are often claimed by pigeon fanciers for their champion racing pigeons, it is unlikely that these birds can exceed 53 mph (85 kph). They are highly prized for their staying power over long distances, however.

Racing pigeon: 53 mph (85 kph)

Duck speed

Ducks are among the fastest birds in level flight, the mallard achieving a top recorded speed of 65 mph (105 kph).

Mallard duck: 65 mph (105 kph)

So fast, it's off the page...

The world's fastest bird – in level flight – is almost twice as fast as any shown here. You'll have to turn to page 42 to find out what it is...

Born to run

The fastest thoroughbred racehorses can gallop at nearly 43 mph (70 kph) over short distances – faster still without jockeys on their backs.

Who needs wings?

Although they are too heavy to fly, adult ostriches can outrun racehorses. Quite small chicks can reach 30 mph (48 kph). In South Africa, ostriches are even raced with jockeys on their backs.

Ostrich: 45 mph (72 kph)

On the hoof

Over short distances, the pronghorn antelope of North America can run more than twice as fast as a charging African elephant.

Pronghorn antelope: 55 mph (88 kph)

On your marks, get set – gone!

The fastest of all land animals, the cheetah, can run at up to 62 mph (100 kph) over short distances. Its amazing acceleration is aided by claws that grip like the spikes of running shoes. If humans ran this fast, the world 100 m record would be a breathtaking 3.6 seconds.

Cheetah: 62 mph (100 kph)

Racehorse: 43 mph (70 kph)

Out of the blue

Speeds of more than 62 mph (100 kph) have been claimed by some people for the American bluefin tuna, but more reliable scientific tests suggest that 46 mph (74 kph) is its top speed.

Bluefin tuna: 46 mph (74 kph)

Marlin: 50 mph (80 kph)

Screaming reels

A favorite catch of deep-sea anglers, the speedy marlin can strip 328 ft (100 m) of line from a fishing reel in less than five seconds.

The fastest fish in the sea

The sailfish is the undisputed ocean sprinting champion, with a recorded peak of 68 mph (110 kph) over short distances. At this speed it could dash the 164-ft (50-m) length of an Olympic swimming pool in only 1.6 seconds – 13 times faster than the quickest human.

Sailfish: 68 mph (110 kph)

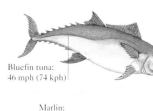

FASTER AND FASTER

RACING A POWERBOAT, driving a fast car, flying a jet – all provide a thrilling dose of speed. In the excitement it is easy to forget that speed is a modern experience. Our ancestors went no faster than they could ride on horseback. For most people the first taste of speed came with railroads. Flight brought even greater speeds, but not right away. When humans first flew, in 1903, the fastest train could do 130 mph (210 kph) – a speed that aircraft did not reach for another 15 years. Space flight is the ultimate thrill. Plummeting back to Earth, the *Apollo 10* astronauts traveled as far in three seconds as they could run in three hours. Space travel is not yet available to all, but long-distance travel on Earth, by land, sea, or air, is now commonplace.

Hopping into the history books

The first powered flight was made in the US, in 1903, by Orville Wright, and lasted an estimated 12 seconds. We will never know exactly how long Orville was airborne, because his brother Wilbur was so excited that he forgot to stop his stopwatch. The brothers did measure the distance of the flight – at 120 ft (37 m), it was less than the wingspan of a jumbo jet.

In August 1960 Joseph Kittinger stepped out of a balloon 102,789 ft (31,330 m) above Tularosa, New Mexico.

Speedy sky divers

Before pulling their rip-cords, sport parachutists relish a few moments of breathtaking speed in free-fall. They accelerate until air resistance stops them from falling faster. Depending on their size, clothing, and posture, they can reach about 121 mph (195 kph). However, plunging from a balloon at 102,789 ft (31,330 m), in 1960, Captain Joseph Kittinger accelerated through the thin air of the upper atmosphere at close to the speed of sound.

In four minutes and 38 seconds, Joseph Kittinger fell 84,711 ft (25,820 m) before his parachute opened – a drop equal to almost 68 Empire State Buildings, or three Mt. Everests.

Empire State Building: 1,250 ft (381 m)

Mt. Everest: 29,028 ft (8,848 m)

The wingspan of a Boeing 747 jumbo jet is 195.5 ft (59.6 m).

On its first flight, the Wright brothers' plane *Flyer* covered only 120 ft (37 m).

Hurrying into the history books

In 1978 Kenneth Warby broke the water speed record on Blowering Dam Lake in his hydroplane *Spirit of Australia*. The custom-made powerboat went fast enough to cover the length of the world's longest river in about 13 hours.

At a top speed of 319 mph (514 kph), *Spirit of Australia* went fast enough to cover the 4,145 miles (6,670 km) of the Nile River in about 13 hours.

Fish left far behind

Measuring the speed of fish is not easy, mainly because no one has yet organized a successful fish race. The gold medal would probably go to the sailfish, which can swim 328 ft (100 m) in little more than three seconds. In a race against *Spirit of Australia*, however, the sailfish would be left trailing.

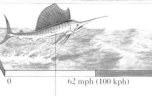

| 0 | 62 mph (100 kph) | 124 mph (200 kph) | 186 mph (300 kph) | 249 mph (400 kph) | 311 mph (500 kph) |

Sailfish: 68 mph (110 kph)

Spirit of Australia: 319 mph (514 kph)

Marathon journeys by sea and air

Tales of long journeys have always had the power to fascinate. Legend has it that, some 2,500 years ago, an unknown messenger ran 22.5 miles (36 km) nonstop to Athens to bring news of a Greek victory on the battlefield at Marathon – a feat commemorated by the road-race of the same name in the Olympic Games. Modern long-distance voyagers set themselves the ultimate challenge: to sail or fly around the world nonstop.

Hi there! By the time we land in Cape Town we will have flown nearly half a million times farther than Orville Wright on his historic first flight!

In Germany, in 1972, Hans-Werner Grosse flew a glider nonstop for a record 908 miles (1,461 km).

In 1967 two Sikorsky HH-3E helicopters flew nonstop from New York to Paris, covering a record 4,271 miles (6,874 km). They took 30 hours and 46 minutes to complete the journey at an average speed of 139 mph (223.5 kph).

In 1981 a helium-filled balloon called *Double Eagle V* flew non-stop from Nagashima, in Japan, to California, covering 5,209 miles (8,383 km). In 1999, the *Breitling Orbiter* completed a record first round-the-world balloon flight, having flown 26,600 miles (42,810 km) in under 20 days.

A Boeing 747 jumbo jet flew nonstop from Paine Field, Washington, to Cape Town, in South Africa, in 1976, covering a record distance for a passenger flight of 10,290 miles (16,560 km).

New York

Paris

On the far side of the Moon

In 1970, the crew of *Apollo 13* traveled the farthest anyone has ever traveled from Earth – 248,671 miles (400,187 km), which is more than 31 times the diameter of the planet. An explosion stopped *Apollo 13* from landing on the Moon. Instead, it had to return to Earth by swinging right around the Moon.

The diameter of the Earth is 7,926 miles (12,756 km).

At its farthest, *Apollo 13* was more than 31 times as far away as the diameter of the Earth.

Jumbo jet lag

At best, a five-hour stagecoach journey in the 18th century might cover a bumpy 37 miles (60 km). Now, allowing for refueling, the Concorde could fly you from London to Singapore in five hours. By jumbo jet, it actually takes more than twice as long, and while the flight might be smooth, you suffer jet lag – tiredness caused by flying between very different time zones – for days afterward.

In five hours, cruising at 1,354 mph (2,179 kph), the Concorde could fly the 6,743 miles (10,852 km) between London and Singapore – about the same time it took an 18th-century stagecoach to cover 37 miles (60 km). If the Concorde took off at 13:00 in London, therefore, it would be about 18:00 in London when it landed – in Singapore, however, it would be about 02:30 in the morning.

In five hours a Lamborghini *Diablo* – at 202 mph (325 kph) the world's fastest road car – could cover the 951 miles (1,531 km) from Rome to Copenhagen, Denmark.

Rome   Copenhagen

0   621 miles (1,000 km)

In five hours a French *TGV* high-speed train – top speed 320 mph (515 kph) – could cover the 1,545 miles (2,486 km) between Paris and Moscow.

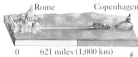

Paris   Moscow

0   621 miles   1,243 miles (2,000 km)
(1,000 km)

London

0   621 miles (1,000 km)   1,864 miles (3,000 km)   3,107 miles (5,000 km)   4,350 miles (7,000 km)   5,592 miles (9,000 km)   Singapore

Making tracks

In 1891 the Russian tsar began to build a railroad line crossing his vast empire. Track was laid from both ends – west from Nakhodka, on the Sea of Japan, and east from Moscow. The world's longest continuous railroad line, it goes nearly a quarter of the way around the globe.

Paris

0   1,243 miles (2,000 km)   2,486 miles (4,000 km)   3,728 miles (6,000 km)   4,971 miles (8,000 km)   Los Angeles

The Earth's equator measures 24,902 miles (40,075 km). Totaling 5,865 miles (9,438 km), the Trans-Siberian Railway stretches a quarter of the way around the world. It was finished in 1916, just one year before the Russian Revolution toppled the tsar.

The Trans-Siberian Railway is longer than the shortest distance between Paris and Los Angeles – 5,645 miles (9,085 km).

Supersonic flyers

"Supersonic" means faster than sound. Sound travels more slowly through the cool, thin air of the upper atmosphere. For aircraft, 660 mph (1,062 kph), or Mach 1, is used as the standard speed of sound at altitude. Mach 2 is twice the speed of sound, and so on.

Sound: Mach 1

Bell X-1 rocket plane: Mach 1

Lockheed SR71A: Mach 3

X-15A-2: Mach 6

Apollo 10 at reentry: Mach 37

0   621 mph (1,000 kph)   1,864 mph (3,000 kph)   3,107 mph (5,000 kph)   4,350 mph (7,000 kph)   18,642 mph (30,000 kph)

Crossing America from coast to coast

American settlers heading west in their wagons in the 1840s and 1850s took about six hazardous months to cross the US. Now the return journey can be done in air-conditioned comfort and safety in less than five hours by jumbo jet.

At 3.7 mph (6 kph) it would take 31 days and 9 hours to walk 2,807 miles (4,517 km), the distance between San Francisco and New York.

At 608 mph (978 kph) a jumbo jet can cover the distance between San Francisco and New York in 4 hours and 38 minutes.

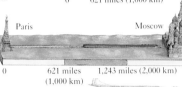

At 4,534 mph (7,297 kph) the X-15A-2 rocket plane could cover the distance between San Francisco and New York in less than 38 minutes.

San Francisco   31 mph (50 kph)   93 mph (150 kph)   559 mph (900 kph)   3,107 mph (5,000 kph)   New York

At 21 mph (34 kph) a stagecoach would take 5 days and 13 hours to travel 2,807 miles (4,517 km).

At 45 mph (72 kph) it would take a 1923 Model T Ford 2 days and 15 hours to travel 2,807 miles (4,517 km).

At 103 mph (165 kph) the *Empire State Express* could travel the distance from San Francisco to New York in less than 28 hours.

In 1986 a specially built plane, *Voyager*, became the first to fly nonstop around the world without refueling. It landed back in California 9 days, 3 minutes, and 44 seconds after taking off.

GRAF ZEPPELIN

Graf Zeppelin was the first rigid airship to fly all the way around the world, in August 1929. It arrived back in New Jersey 21 days, 5 hours, and 31 minutes after setting out, having flown at least 21,873 miles (35,200 km).

In 1968-69, in his boat *Suhaili*, Robin Knox-Johnson became the first person to sail, single-handedly, nonstop around the world. He covered a total of 30,122 miles (48,478 km) in 312 days.

12,428 miles (20,000 km)   15,535 miles (25,000 km)   18,642 miles (30,000 km)   21,749 miles (35,000 km)

AIR SPEED

HISTORY WAS MADE one winter morning in 1903 when two American bicycle mechanics towed a fragile timber and cloth aircraft onto a sandy North Carolina beach, started its noisy engine, and flew. The Wright brothers, Wilbur and Orville, were the world's first pilots, but their *Flyer* would have won no prizes for speed. It flew at only 30 mph (48 kph), and on its longest flight, took nearly one minute to cover only 852 ft (260 m). In 1967, only 64 years after the Wright brothers first flew, the X-15A-2 rocket plane flew more than 150 times faster. In the 59 seconds that the *Flyer* was airborne at Kitty Hawk, the X-15A-2 could have flown past Norfolk, Virginia, some 75 miles (120 km) away.

Speedy Spitfire

At the start of World War II (1939-45), the British Supermarine Spitfire was the world's fastest fighter aircraft. The fastest Spitfire, the Mk XIV, flew four times as fast as the natural world's fastest flyer, the spine-tailed swift.

Wright kite

The Wright brothers chose North Carolina's Outer Banks as the site to test their *Flyer* because the strong, steady winds there helped lift the aircraft into the air, like a kite.

Westland *Lynx*:
249 mph (400 kph)

Three-winged fighter

Although no faster than the world's fastest bird, the Fokker Dr.I triplane was one of the most successful German fighter aircraft of World War I (1914-18). Flying a red-painted model, Manfred von Richthofen, the famous Red Baron, shot down 80 enemy planes.

Chop, chop!

The world's fastest helicopter, the Westland *Lynx*, can fly at up to 249 mph (400 kph) – almost 14 times faster than the world's fastest insects, dragonflies. However, in normal use and fully loaded with 10 troops or two torpedoes, it cruises at about two-thirds of that speed.

Supermarine
Spitfire Mk XIV:
448 mph (721 kph)

Flyer:
30 mph
(48 kph)

Fokker Dr.I:
103 mph (165 kph)

Dawdling doodlebugs

V1 flying bombs, or doodlebugs, developed by Germany during World War II, were pilotless aircraft laden with explosives. Slower than fighter planes, they could be shot down, and less than half reached their targets.

V1 flying bomb:
350 mph
(563 kph)

Stately pioneer

Although slower than the top speed of a modern car, the *Hindenburg* airship was the world's first transatlantic passenger service by air, crossing between Germany and the US.

Hindenburg: cruising speed 78 mph (126 kph)

Silent swoopers

Gliders are unpowered aircraft that soar on rising currents of warm air. They can swoop at up to 199 mph (320 kph) – faster than the fastest motorcycle – but cruise at half this speed.

Swift birds

Spine-tailed swifts can fly faster than any aircraft built before World War I.

Glider:
199 mph
(320 kph)

Spine-tailed swift:
106 mph (171 kph)

Feathered flight

A skilled archer can fire a longbow arrow fast enough to spear the world's fastest helicopter.

Longbow arrow:
342 mph (550 kph)

Keep pedaling!

Human-powered aircraft have huge wings to lift them into the air at very low speeds. In 1979, Bryan Allen pedaled *Gossamer Albatross* across the English Channel so slowly – at half the speed of the Wright brothers' *Flyer* – that it barely cleared the waves.

Gossamer Albatross:
15 mph (24 kph)

Plunging birds

Peregrine falcons can dive as fast as the landing speed of a space shuttle.

Peregrine falcons can dive at 217 mph (350 kph).

Super seaplane

From 1913-31, competition for the Schneider Trophy for seaplanes repeatedly raised the air speed record. After winning the final contest as the only entrant, the British Supermarine S.6B set a record of 379 mph (610 kph) – faster than a speeding arrow. Two weeks later it broke the 400 mph (644 kph) barrier. It was later modified into the Spitfire fighter.

Touchdown!

The speed of a space shuttle on landing is more than three times as fast as the top speed of the fastest land animal on Earth, the cheetah.

Space shuttle:
landing speed 217 mph (350 kph)

Cheetah: 62 mph (100 kph)

Supermarine S.6B
407 mph (655 kph

| 0 | 62 mph (100 kph) | 124 mph (200 kph) | 186 mph (300 kph) | 249 mph (400 kph) | 311 mph (500 kph) | 373 mph (600 kph) |

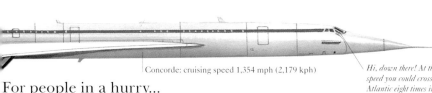

Concorde: cruising speed 1,354 mph (2,179 kph)

For people in a hurry...

The Concorde is the world's fastest passenger aircraft. Holding up to 130 passengers, it can fly from New York to London in under three hours. The same journey takes more than twice as long in an ordinary passenger aircraft.

Hi, down there! At this speed you could cross the Atlantic eight times in one day – although after the first few times, you wouldn't know if you were coming or going!

X-15A-2 tops the lot

The fastest aircraft of all time, the 1960s North American X-15A-2 did not take off from a runway in the conventional way. Instead, a B-52 bomber ferried it to its cruising altitude, where its rocket engines blasted it to a maximum speed more than 150 times as fast as the Wright brothers' *Flyer*.

X-15A-2: maximum speed 4,534 mph (7,297 kph)

Yeager goes supersonic

Until the 1940s, many people believed that it would be impossible to fly faster than the speed of sound – about 764 mph (1,229 kph) near the ground, and 660 mph (1,062 kph) in the thinner upper atmosphere. Then, in 1947, American pilot Charles Yeager broke the sound barrier – Mach 1 – in a specially built, rocket-powered aircraft, the Bell X-1. Like the later X-15A and X-15A-2, the Bell X-1 was launched high in the air from a bomber.

Bell X-1: 701 mph (1,128 kph)

V2 rocket: 3,542 mph (5,700 kph)

Rocket bombs

Pioneering German rocket engineers built 3,610 V2 missiles toward the end of World War II. Aimed at cities, V2s traveled more than twice as fast as an ordinary rifle bullet.

Lockheed SR71A: 2,193 mph (3,530 kph)

Blackbird scorches speed record

The world air speed record for an aircraft taking off from the ground was set by the US Air Force in a Lockheed SR71A spy plane, in 1976. Nicknamed *Blackbird*, it flew more than 70 times as fast as the Wright brothers' *Flyer*.

Up, up, and away!

Aviators aiming for record heights quickly run out of air. Balloonists need it to buoy up their gas-filled envelopes. Pilots control their aircraft using the flow of air over rudders, ailerons, and elevators. The record breaking X-15A used tiny rockets for extra control in the thin air of the upper atmosphere.

Boeing 747: cruising speed 608 mph (978 kph)

Cruising the skies

Boeing 747 jumbo jet passenger planes cruise at close to the speed of sound, and more than seven times as fast as the *Hindenburg* airship.

In August 1963, American test pilot Joseph Walker flew his X-15A over Edwards Air Force Base to 354,200 ft (107,960 m) – more than 12 times the height of Mt. Everest.

Foxbat flies flat-out

Although designed back in the 1960s, the Russian MiG-25 is still the world's fastest combat aircraft. Nicknamed *Foxbat*, it can fly almost 10 times as fast as a diving peregrine falcon.

MiG-25: 2,110 mph (3,395 kph)

In May 1961, Malcolm Ross and Victor Prather rose in a gas balloon from the deck of the USS *Antietam* to 113,740 ft (34,668 m) above the Gulf of Mexico – almost four times the height of Mt. Everest.

Fighter folds its wings

The main European combat aircraft, the Panavia *Tornado*, has wings that fold back during supersonic flight, much like the wings of a swooping spine-tailed swift. The *Tornado* is almost 14 times faster, however.

Tornado: 1,465 mph (2,357 kph)

Jet jumps into the air

By pointing the jet nozzles of the BAe *Harrier* downward, the pilot can take off vertically, just like a bird. Swiveled to the horizontal position, the nozzles thrust the fighter plane forward at more than the speed of sound.

BAe *Harrier*: 739 mph (1,190 kph)

Shooting ahead

An ordinary rifle bullet flies fast enough to put a hole in all but the world's fastest fighter aircraft.

Back to the drawing board...

Power for the tiny Messerschmitt 163 *Komet* came from a single rocket, which accelerated it to almost twice the speed of an arrow. The plane had little impact on World War II, however, because it was uncontrollable at top speed, and ran out of fuel after only 10 minutes.

Me 163 *Komet*: 624 mph (1,004 kph)

Rifle bullet: 1,637 mph (2,635 kph)

Mt. Everest: 29,028 ft (8,848 m)

GREAT CAPACITIES

IT IS EASIER TO GRASP the widths, heights, and lengths of things than it is to imagine their volumes and capacities – the amount of space they contain, and how much of something it takes to fill that space. The reason is simple: when the width, height, and length of something doubles, its volume increases eightfold. This rule explains the almost unbelievable fact that the fleet of trucks required to deliver enough standard containers to fill the huge Vehicle Assembly Building at the Kennedy Space Center would stretch from Paris to Rome. It also explains the equally amazing fact that just one water tower can hold enough water for someone to take a bath every day of the year for 65 years.

In case of another oil shortage...

Saudi Arabia is the world's largest oil producer, so it is not surprising that it also has the world's largest oil storage facilities. Each of the five colossal oil tanks at Ju'aymah is taller than a four-story town house and wider than the length of a soccer field. Each can hold 81,232,890 gallons (307,500,000 liters), or 1,500,000 barrels, of oil. If the oil were gasoline, each tank could hold enough for the average car to drive to the Moon and back about 6,000 times.

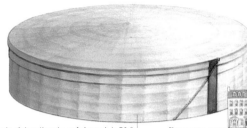

Each of the oil tanks at Ju'aymah is 72 ft (22 m) high and 387 ft (118 m) wide.

Four-story town house: 66 ft (20 m) tall

One very big refinery

The largest oil refinery in the world is in Judibana, Falcón, Venezuela. The *Petroleos de Venezuela* can process 28,702,288 gallons (108,650,000 liters), or 530,000 barrels, of crude oil a day – one barrel being 54 gallons (205 liters). In one year, this is equivalent to refining all the oil in 61 large supertankers, each holding about 171,711,800 gallons (650,000,000 liters), or about 3,170,000 barrels – more than one supertanker a week.

In a year, *Petroleos de Venezuela* could process 193,450,000 barrels of crude oil.

Sixty-one large supertankers could carry 193,370,000 barrels of crude oil.

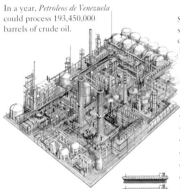

Supertankers swallow storage tanks

Even bigger than the largest container ships, the largest supertankers in the world can hold about 171,711,800 gallons (650,000,000 liters), or about 3,170,000 barrels, of oil – more than twice as much as one of the five giant storage tanks at Ju'aymah, in Saudi Arabia.

Two Ju'aymah tanks: 3,000,000 barrels of oil

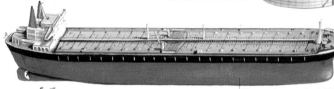

Supertankers can be 1,591 ft (485 m) long and 230 ft (70 m) wide, and can carry 3,170,000 barrels of oil.

Four-story town house: 66 ft (20 m) tall

Dresden Express, one of the world's largest container ships, is 965 ft (294 m) long and 131 ft (40 m) wide.

Space center has truckloads of room

Built in 1965 for the huge *Saturn V* rockets, the Vehicle Assembly Building at the Kennedy Space Center, in Florida, is one of the largest buildings in the world. It is 715 ft (218 m) long and 518 ft (158 m) wide, with one bay 525 ft (160 m) high, and another bay 210 ft (64 m) high. Its total volume is 129,428,128 cubic ft (3,664,993 cubic m) – room enough to stack about 100,000 standard containers. Were all the containers to be delivered on the same day, the line of trucks would stretch about as far as the distance from Paris to Rome.

One of the Vehicle Assembly Building's two bays is 525 ft (160 m) high.

Bath time – again

The waterspheroid water tower in Edmond, Oklahoma, holds 500,077 gallons (1,893,000 liters) when full. Allowing 21 gallons (80 liters) for a bath, that is enough water for an amazing 23,663 baths – one every day of the year for 65 years.

Edmond waterspheroid: 161 ft (49 m) tall

Hi! Only 23,662 more to go... I wonder if I've got enough soap?

Four-story town house: 66 ft (20 m)

Each tub represents about 500 baths

The Edmond waterspheroid can hold enough water for 23,663 baths.

Carrying containers by the thousands

Bulk products such as coal and wheat are carried loose in dry-cargo ships, but valuable goods such as clothes and electronic equipment are carried in container ships. Sealed metal containers allow all sorts of goods to be carried, without damage, by sea. Refrigerated containers allow even perishable goods, such as meat, to be carried all around the world. The more containers a ship can carry, the cheaper it is to move each container. Built in 1991, *Dresden Express*, one of the largest container ships in the world, has an overall capacity of 4,422 standard containers.

Dresden Express

Container truck

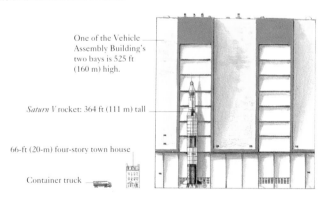

Saturn V rocket: 364 ft (111 m) tall

66-ft (20-m) four-story town house

Container truck

A standard container is 20 ft (6 m) long, 8 ft (2.4 m) high, and 8 ft (2.4 m) wide, and is about 1,271 cubic ft (36 cubic m).

Paris

Allowing slightly more than 33 ft (10 m) for each truck, 100,000 standard container trucks would stretch about as far as the 687 miles (1,105 km) from Paris to Rome.

Rome

Built in the 1930s, *Graf Zeppelin II* was 804 ft (245 m) long, and held almost 7,062,940 cubic ft (200,000 cubic m) of hydrogen. (Her sister airship, *Hindenburg*, was just as big.)

Gigantic gas holder

The world's largest gas holder, at Simmering, Vienna, Austria, is as tall as the largest living thing on Earth, the General Sherman giant sequoia. When full, it holds enough gas to fill either of the two largest airships ever built one-and-a-half times over. The same amount of gas could also fill four of the biggest-ever hot-air balloons, or 138 ordinary hot-air balloons.

Four-story town house: 66 ft (20 m) tall

The General Sherman giant sequoia, in California, is 276 ft (84 m) tall.

The Simmering gas holder is 276 ft (84 m) tall and holds 10,594,410 cubic ft (300,000 cubic m) of gas when full.

One of the largest hot-air balloons ever flown, the *Virgin Otsuka Pacific Flyer*, held 2,600,009 cubic ft (73,624 cubic m) of hot air. Richard Branson and Per Lindstrand flew it across the Pacific Ocean in 1991.

A standard hot-air balloon holds 76,986 cubic ft (2,180 cubic m) of hot air.

By the busload

The capacity of buses varies around the world, but 49 passengers is about average.

The average bus can hold 49 passengers.

Almost 12 busloads of people are needed to fill a jumbo jet, at its maximum capacity.

By the jetload

The number of passenger seats that a Boeing 747 jumbo jet contains varies from airline to airline, and depends on the type of seats, how the seats are arranged, and the amount of room allowed for each passenger. The maximum number, however, is 570 – almost 12 busloads.

The maximum passenger capacity of a jumbo jet is 570.

By the boatload

In addition to 350 cars and 60 trucks, the *Silja Europa* ferry, which operates between Finland and Sweden, can carry up to 3,000 passengers – more than five times as many as a jumbo jet.

The *Silja Europa* ferry is 98 ft (30 m) wide and 656 ft (200 m) long. It can hold 3,000 passengers.

It would take more than five jumbo-jetloads of passengers to fill the *Silja Europa* ferry.

Pulling in the crowds

The *Circus Maximus* arena of ancient Rome is said to have held upward of 250,000 people. The largest stadium in the modern world, the open Strahov Stadium, in Prague, in the Czech Republic, could hold about 240,000 spectators when it was completed in 1934 – more than twice as many as the world's biggest covered stadiums. It was built to accommodate mass gymnastics displays featuring up to 40,000 people performing in unison. To fill the Strahov Stadium would require 80 full *Silja Europa* ferries...or 421 full jumbo jets...or 4,898 full buses.

When completed in 1934, the Strahov Stadium could hold 240,000 spectators.

It would take 80 full *Silja Europa* ferries to fill the Strahov Stadium.

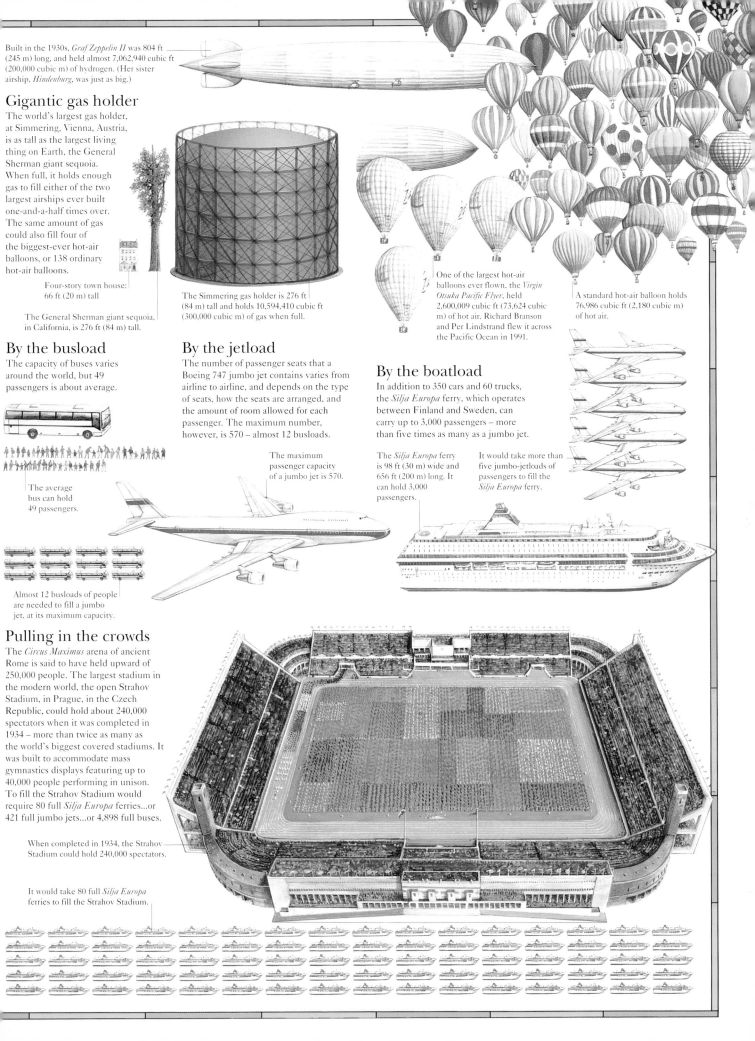

BIG BUILDINGS

THE WORLD'S TALLEST buildings are the twin structures of the 1,482-ft (452-m) Petronas Towers, in Kuala Lumpur, Malaysia, opened in 1996. They overtook the 110-story Sears Tower in Chicago. Even taller buildings are planned around the world, although work on several in Asia has been suspended for economic reasons. Among these is the Shanghai World Financial Center in Shanghai, China; if completed, its 94 storeys will soar to 460 m (1,509 ft). But there are even higher structures, such as television towers. These are so tall that they are not self-supporting – they are held up with strong cables called guy wires. The tallest structure ever built was a television tower near Warsaw, Poland. It was a cloud-tickling 2,119 ft (646 m), but fell in 1991 while it was being repaired. Today, the world's tallest structure is the KTHI-TV tower in North Dakota.

Four-story town house:
66 ft (20 m)

Head for heights
A four-story town house is like a doll's house compared with the Statue of Liberty.

Viewing gallery in head

Statue of Liberty: 75 ft (23 m) from shoulders to torch

The corridors of power
St. Peter's church would fit twice into the ground area occupied by the Great Pyramid. But both buildings are dwarfed by the vast floor area of the Pentagon, a government building in Washington, DC. With its maze of corridors, the five-sided Pentagon is the largest office complex in the world.

Hi there – I'm lost! There are about 17 miles (27 km) of corridors here. That's a minimum four-hour walk. Help!

Pentagon: 1,263,240 sq ft (117,355 sq m)

Great Pyramid: 571,530 sq ft (53,095 sq m)

St. Peter's: 392,310 sq ft (36,446 sq m)

Packing them in
Modern office buildings are designed to hold many people on large floor areas. If you draw St. Peter's, the Empire State Building, and one of the two World Trade Center towers in proportion to how many people each can hold, you get this result:

World Trade Center tower: Completed 1973 Holds 25,000 people

Empire State Building: Completed 1931 Holds 15,000 people

St. Peter's: Completed 1590 Holds 3,000 people

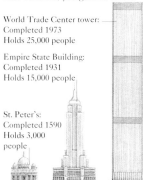
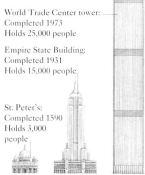

Built to last
The Great Pyramid is almost entirely solid, so an immense amount of stone was used to build it – more than 90 million cubic ft (2.5 million cubic m). The same volume of brick and stone would build 40 Empire State Buildings.

40 Empire State Buildings

1 Great Pyramid

High office
At 797 ft (243 m), 1 Canada Square, at Canary Wharf, in London, is the UK's tallest office building. A chain of 8,000 paper clips dangled from the top floor would just about reach the ground.

1 Canada Square

Twin peaks
Cologne Cathedral, in Germany, has twin spires that are each 513 ft (156 m) high. When built, in the 1880s, they were the world's tallest artificial structures.

High church
With its enormous dome, St. Peter's, in Rome, rises to 451 ft (137.5 m) – almost the length of two jumbo jets.

Desert wonder
It would take about 70 camels standing on each other's backs to reach the top of the Great Pyramid, at Giza, in Egypt. Built some 4,500 years ago as the tomb of King Khufu, it is 481 ft (147 m) high.

Toppling tower
At 180 ft (55 m), the famous Leaning Tower of Pisa, in Italy, is nearly three times as high as a four-story town house.

Lofty statue
The Statue of Liberty, in New York, is 305 ft (93 m) high from the base of the pedestal to the torch.

Four-story town house: 66 ft (20 m)

Leaning Tower

St. Peter's

Statue of Liberty

Missing top stone included in height

Great Pyramid

Cologne Cathedral

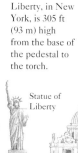

1,969 ft (600 m)

1,640 ft (500 m)

1,312 ft (400 m)

984 ft (300 m)

656 ft (200 m)

328 ft (100 m)

0

Put in their place

Compared with the world's great mountain ranges, such as the lofty Himalayas, even the tallest buildings are really very small indeed. It would take no fewer than 27 Eiffel Towers stacked one on top of the other to reach the peak of Mt. Everest, the world's highest mountain. Even the tallest artificial structure in the world, North Dakota's KTHI-TV tower, would fit 14 times into the height of Everest. As for 66-ft (20-m), four-story town houses, you would need no fewer than 443 of them to reach the top of the world's highest mountain.

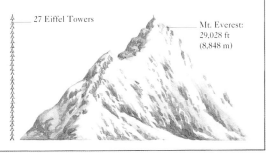

27 Eiffel Towers

Mt. Everest: 29,028 ft (8,848 m)

On a high wire

The KTHI-TV tower, in North Dakota, rises to a height of 2,063 ft (629 m). Supported by guy wires, it is the world's tallest artificial structure.

KTHI-TV tower

Standing tall

The world's highest self-supporting tower, at 1,815 ft (553 m), is the CN Tower, in Toronto. It is five times as tall as the world's tallest tree.

THE ONLY WAY IS UP

Great advances in engineering mean modern buildings can be much taller than those of past centuries. Older buildings have solid, heavy walls, but today's skyscrapers have lightweight outer frameworks of steel and glass. The tallest modern buildings are in city centers. So many people want to live and work in city centers that skyscrapers are the only way to fit everyone in.

It's official

For many years the world's tallest office building was the Sears Tower, in Chicago, at 443 m (1,453 ft) high – four times as tall as a *Saturn V* rocket.

High fliers

The World Trade Center, in New York, has two towers, the taller of which rises to 1,375 ft (419 m).

Celebrity 'scraper

The world's best-known skyscraper is the 102-story Empire State Building, in New York. It is 1,250 ft (381 m) tall, not counting the mast. Like other skyscrapers, it has warning beacons for low-flying aircraft.

Corporate structure

The Chrysler Building, in New York, is 1,046 ft (319 m) high to the top of its spire – equivalent to 60 of the city's famous yellow taxicabs stuck bumper to bumper in a traffic jam.

High finance

It would take a stack of 8,268 standard size (1.5-in/3.81-cm high) gold bars to reach the top of the 1,033-ft (315-m) tall Bank of China Building, in Hong Kong.

Towering success

At 1,052 ft (321 m) tall – including the radio mast – the Eiffel Tower, in Paris, is 16 times as tall as a 66-ft (20-m), four-story town house. It was built for the 1889 Paris Exhibition, and remains a popular tourist attraction.

I'm on the tower's second level. Only 952 more steps to the top – I think I'll take the elevator!

CN Tower

Sears Tower

World Trade Center

Empire State Building

Chrysler Building

Bank of China Building

Eiffel Tower

1,969 ft (600 m)

1,640 ft (500 m)

1,312 ft (400 m)

984 ft (300 m)

656 ft (200 m)

328 ft (100 m)

0

Four-story town house

Saturn V rocket: 364 ft (111 m)

HUMAN POPULATION

A POPULATION EXPLOSION has seen the number of people in the world more than triple since 1900 – from less than 2,000,000,000 to more than 6,000,000,000 at the end of the 20th century. Each day, enough people to fill the largest stadium in the modern world are added to the total. Thankfully, the world is a very big place. All the people in the world today could actually fit, standing shoulder to shoulder, on the small Indonesian island of Bali. Most of the world is only sparsely inhabited, and there are more people in some cities than there are in some of the largest countries. But nowhere do you find more people than in China – 20 percent of all the people in the world live in this huge country.

Of the 6,000,000,000 or so people in the world, 1,256,000,000 live in China. This means that, worldwide, almost one person in five lives in China.

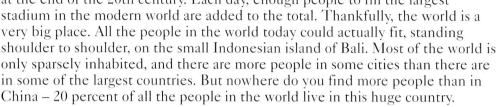

China grows and grows

China's population is bigger than that of any other country. Government policies now restrict couples in China from having more than one child, but even so it is predicted that the country's population will reach 1,477,730,000 by the year 2050.

There are more people in China today than there were in the whole world as recently as 150 years ago.

China, the US, and Australia mapped in proportion to their populations

Only about 18,500,000 people live in Australia, mainly in coastal cities. Large areas of this vast country are desert.

The population of the US (including Alaska and Hawaii) is about 274,000,000 – 15 times bigger than that of Australia.

China's population of 1,256,000,000 is almost five times bigger than that of the US, and 68 times bigger than that of Australia.

China's population in perspective

China covers an area only slightly greater than that of the US, while Australia is not far behind China and the US as one of the world's largest countries. However, the population of China is nearly five times greater than that of the US, and an amazing 67 times greater than that of Australia. When the maps of these three countries are redrawn to a scale in proportion to their populations, rather than their actual areas, you can see just how vast the population of China really is.

Australia is the fifth largest country in the world – after Russia, Canada, China, and the US – but has a population no bigger than that of Sri Lanka.

Land and people...

Japan and Zimbabwe are countries with almost exactly the same land areas, but with very different populations. In terms of population, it would take 11.5 Zimbabwes to equal one Japan.

The population of Japan is about 126,000,000.

The population of Zimbabwe is about 11,000,000.

People and land...

Australia and Sri Lanka are countries with similar populations, but Sri Lanka would fit into Australia 119 times. If Australia were as densely populated as Sri Lanka, Australia's population would be more than 2,000,000,000. If Sri Lanka were as sparsely populated as Australia, Sri Lanka's population would be only about 150,000.

The population of Sri Lanka is about 18,000,000.

Size by area

In this box, all the countries featured on these two pages are drawn in proportion to their actual size in area.

China: 3,705,676 sq miles (9,596,960 sq km)

US: 3,679,459 sq miles (9,529,063 sq km)

Australia: 3,026,044 sq miles (7,836,848 sq km)

Sudan: 967,570 sq miles (2,505,813 sq km)

Japan: 145,880 sq miles (377,800 sq km)

Sri Lanka: 25,334 sq miles (65,610 sq km)

Zimbabwe: 150,815 sq miles (390,580 sq km)

South Korea: 38,235 sq miles (99,020 sq km)

Bali: 2,170 sq miles (5,620 sq km)

Population pyramids

Living standards in a country are reflected in the age structure of its population. In poor countries, families tend to be large, but few people survive to old age. In rich countries, by contrast, families tend to be small, and better living conditions mean that many more people survive to old age. The difference is clear if you look at the age structures of Rwanda, a poor country, and Sweden, a rich one, as "population pyramids." These two countries have similar total populations, but very different numbers of young and old people.

Age 75+: 50,000 (0.6%)
Age 60-74: 270,000 (3.4%)
Age 45-59: 591,000 (7.5%)
Age 30-44: 1,095,000 (14%)
Age 15-29: 2,150,000 (27.5%)
Age 0-14: 3,651,000 (47%)

RWANDA
(population 7,807,000)

Age 75+: 715,000 (8%)
Age 60-74: 1,223,000 (14%)
Age 45-59: 1,685,000 (19%)
Age 30-44: 1,790,000 (20.5%)
Age 15-29: 1,720,000 (19.5%)
Age 0-14: 1,652,000 (19%)

SWEDEN
(population 8,785,000)

Crowding the court

All cities are crowded, but some are more crowded than others. Take the population densities of London and Hong Kong Island. Hong Kong Island is so closely packed that if it were divided into tennis courts, there would be 25 people on each court. In London there would be only one person on each court.

Hong Kong Island: 25 people in an area the size of a tennis court

A tennis court covers 2,808 sq ft (261 sq m).

London: one person in an area the size of a tennis court

The world on an island

Allowing about 10.8 sq ft (1 sq m) per person, all the people in the world could stand shoulder to shoulder on the Indonesian island of Bali. The biggest problem would be getting them all there...

Bali has an area of about 60,495,156,000 sq ft (5,620,000,000 sq m) – slightly less than 10.8 sq ft (1 sq m) for each of the 5,734,000,000 people on Earth.

Stop shoving, will you? There's plenty of room!

Accelerated growth

The population of the world in 1500 was about 460,000,000, after centuries of slow growth. It then grew steadily until the middle of the 19th century, when it passed 1,000,000,000. It then began the incredible rise that has already enlarged it to more than 12 times the 1500 figure. In another 100 years it could almost double, to close to 11,000,000,000.

Colossal conurbation

When two or more cities grow until they merge, they form a conurbation. The population of the conurbation of Tokyo and Yokahama, in Japan, is about as big as the population of Sudan, a large country that is mainly uninhabited desert.

The population of Sudan is about 28,000,000.

Tokyo and Yokohama conurbation: population about 28,000,000

Seoul: population more than 19,000,000

City outgrows Australia

Seoul, the capital of South Korea, is one of the largest and fastest growing cities in the world, with a population greater than that of the whole of Australia.

There are fewer people in the whole of Australia than there are in Seoul.

A new crowd every day

Worldwide, on average, 382,650 babies are born and 144,902 people die every day. This means that, on average, the population of the world increases by 237,748 each day. That is almost enough people to fill the largest stadium in the modern world, the Strahov Stadium, in Prague, Czech Republic.

Each day, the world's population increases by nearly 240,000 – equivalent to one full Strahov Stadium.

Bali

The Indonesian island of Bali would fit more than 1,394 times into Australia.

World population in 1995: 5,734,000,000

World population in 1985: 4,854,000,000

World population in 1980: 4,450,000,000

World population in 1970: 3,698,000,000

World population in 1960: 3,019,000,000

World population in 1950: 2,515,000,000

World population in 1900: 1,633,000,000

World population in 1850: 1,094,000,000

World population in 1800: 954,000,000

World population in 1700: 679,000,000

World population in 1600: 579,000,000

World population in 1500: 460,000,000

World population: expected to reach 11,000,000,000 in 2093, then level out

World population: expected to reach 10,000,000,000 in 2054, then grow much more slowly in the second half of the 21st century

World population: expected to reach 9,000,000,000 in 2035

World population: expected to reach 8,000,000,000 in 2021

World population: expected to reach 7,000,000,000 in 2009

World population: exceeded 6,000,000,000 in 1999

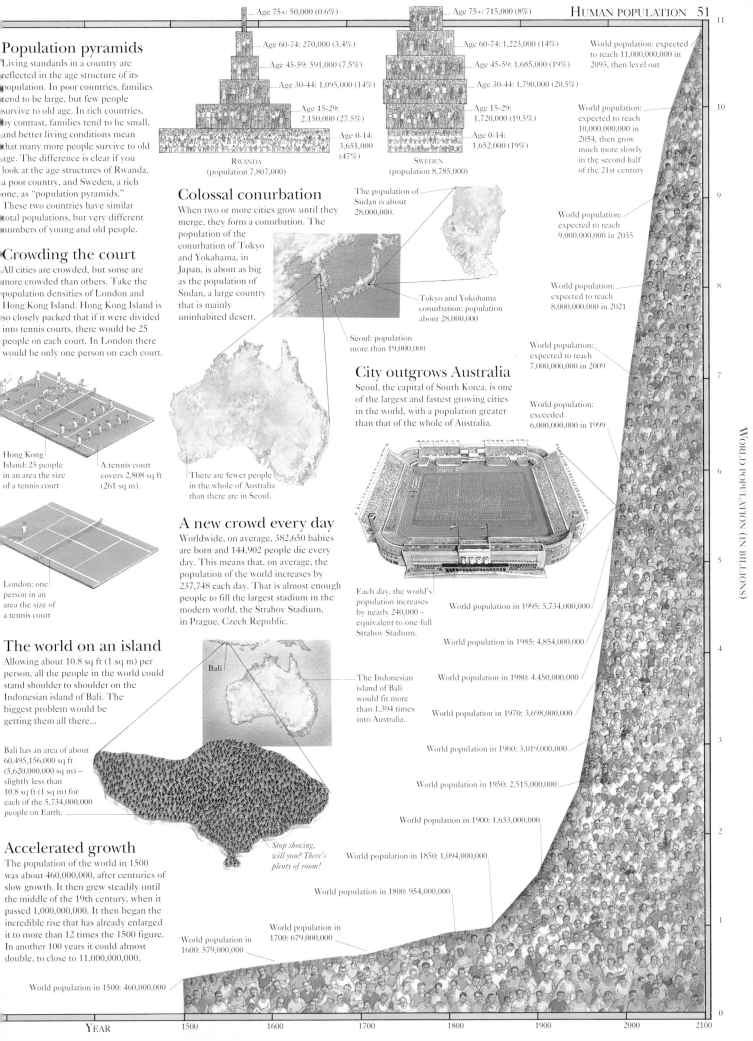

WORLD POPULATION (IN BILLIONS)

YEAR
1500 1600 1700 1800 1900 2000 2100

GROWTH AND AGE

"GREAT OAKS FROM little acorns grow." It is one of the marvels of nature that nearly all living things increase in size, often by a phenomenal factor of many millions from the seed or egg from which they originated. This growth can be extremely rapid and quite short-lived, or it can be very slow and extended over many years – over many centuries, even. Bamboo can grow as much in one day as one species of evergreen shrub might grow in 1,000 or more years. No animal lives anywhere near as long as the longest-lived trees or plants. Given the right conditions, however, some creatures can live for a surprisingly long time – including humans, for whom a life span of 100 years is nowadays by no means unusual.

Bamboo shoots up twice as fast

Pacific giant kelp, a kind of seaweed, can grow as much as 18 in (45 cm) in one day. If you think that is a lot, then try bamboo. Bamboo can grow at twice that rate – by the height of an average two-year-old child in one day. Bamboo grows fast because it is actually a kind of grass found in tropical and semi-tropical countries where there is a very high rainfall. Just think how the grass always seems to need cutting after a downpour. Bamboo might grow twice as fast as Pacific giant kelp, but the kelp can eventually grow to twice the size of bamboo – and 34 times the height of the average man.

Pacific giant kelp can grow 18 in (45 cm) in one day.

Bamboo can grow 3 ft (90 cm) in one day.

The average two-year-old child is 2 ft 9 in (84 cm) tall.

High and mighty

The tallest tree in the world is a coast redwood, in the Humboldt Redwoods State Park, California. Standing 363 ft (110.6 m) high, it is 58 ft (17.6 m) taller than the Statue of Liberty and nearly twice as big as fully grown Pacific giant kelp. Much taller eucalyptus trees were recorded in Australia in the 19th century, however – trees more than 426 ft (130 m) high.

Coast redwood: 363 ft (110.6 m) from base of trunk to top of tree

Statue of Liberty: 305 ft (93 m) from base of pedestal to torch

Shrub grows ever so slowly

A 120-year-old specimen of *Dioon edule*, an evergreen shrub found in Mexico, was just 4 in (10 cm) tall, and growing at an almost imperceptible 0.03 in (0.76 mm) a year. At that rate it would take 1,184 years to grow as much as bamboo can grow in one day.

Pacific giant kelp can grow to 197 ft (60 m) – 34 times the height of the average man.

Bamboo can grow to 98 ft (30 m).

100 years

50 years

I think I'm going to need a bigger lawn mower!

The average man is 5 ft 9 in (1.75 m) tall.

One specimen of *Dioon edule* was found to be growing at only 0.03 in (0.76 mm) a year.

Pacific giant kelp: up to 197 ft (60 m)

Ancient trees outlive humans and animals

Most animals live much longer in captivity than they do in the wild because in captivity they are well fed, receive regular medical attention, and are safe from predators. Over the years, human life expectancy has increased steadily, mainly because of advances in medicine. Today it is highest in rich, industrialized countries with good diets, and lowest in poor countries. We still have a long way to go to catch up to the longest lived trees, however, which can live for 50 times as long as the oldest humans.

Women generally live longer than men. The average life expectancy for women in the US is 75 years, and there are increasing numbers living for more than 100 years.

The average life expectancy for men in the US is 72 years.

Chimpanzee: up to 53 years

Hippopotamus: up to 54 years

Eagle owl: up to 68 years

Indian elephant: up to 77 years

Rhinoceros: up to 50 years

Dolphin: up to 65 years

Mouse: up to 6 years

Trout: up to 10 years

Rabbit: up to 13 years

Dog: up to 20 years

Tiger: up to 26 years

Cow: up to 30 years

Polar bear: up to 38 years

Bison: up to 40 years

0   10 years   20 years   30 years   40 years   50 years   60 years   70 years   80 ye

Growing together

From 20 in (50 cm) and 7.5 lb (3.4 kg) when born, the average human increases in height by slightly more than three times, and increases in weight about 18 times. Although there are slight fluctuations, the growth rates of boys and girls remain similar until early adulthood, when men overtake women.

Female – 6 months: 2 ft 2 in (66 cm) 16 lb (7.2 kg)

Female – 1 year: 2 ft 5 in (74 cm) 20 lb (9.1 kg)

Female – 2 years: 2 ft 9 in (84 cm) 25 lb (11.3 kg)

Female – 6 years: 3 ft 8 in (112 cm) 45 lb (20.4 kg)

Female – 10 years: 4 ft 6 in (137 cm) 69 lb (31.3 kg)

Female – 14 years: 5 ft 2 in (157 cm) 107 lb (48.5 kg)

Female – 18 years: 5 ft 5 in (165 cm) 126 lb (57 kg)

Male – 6 months: 2 ft 2 in (66 cm) 17 lb (7.7 kg)

Male – 1 year: 2 ft 5 in (74 cm) 21 lb (9.5 kg)

Male – 2 years: 2 ft 9 in (84 cm) 26 lb (11.8 kg)

Male – 6 years: 3 ft 9 in (114 cm) 46 lb (20.9 kg)

Male – 10 years: 4 ft 6 in (137 cm) 69 lb (31.3 kg)

Male – 14 years: 5 ft 2 in (157 cm) 107 lb (48.5 kg)

Male – 18 years: 5 ft 9 in (175 cm) 141 lb (64 kg)

Slow clam

Clams are among the longest lived and slowest growing of all creatures. *Tindaria callistiformis*, a deep-sea clam, might take up to 100 years to reach only about 0.3 in (8 mm) in diameter.

Even after growing for 100 years, *Tindaria callistiformis* might fit on your fingernail.

Largest life-form

The biggest living thing on Earth is a tree: the General Sherman giant sequoia, in Sequoia National Park, California. Its base is thicker than a giraffe is tall.

The General Sherman giant sequoia is about 26 ft (8 m) thick at its base.

Giraffe: 19 ft (5.8 m)

Growing up fast

Feeding on its mother's rich milk, a blue whale calf can gain 139 lb (63 kg) a day in its first year, and grow to nearly nine times its birth weight. A baby increasing its 7.5 lb (3.4 kg) birth weight by nearly nine times would weigh almost as much as a 10-year-old child after one year.

At birth a blue whale calf weighs up to 3 tons (3 tonnes).

After only one year a blue whale can weigh 29 tons (26 tonnes).

10-year-old girl: 69 lb (31.3 kg)

1-year-old girl: 20 lb (9.1 kg)

Crocodile man?

A 10-in (26-cm) baby Nile crocodile can grow 19 times as long, to become a 16-ft 5-in (5-m) adult. If humans grew like this, a 20-in (50-cm) baby would grow into a 31-ft (9.5-m) adult – more than five times as tall as the average man.

If humans grew like Nile crocodiles, a 20-in (50-cm) baby would grow up to become a 31-ft (9.5-m) giant.

16-ft 5-in (5-m) Nile crocodile

5-ft 9-in (1.75-m) man

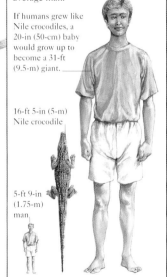

The General Sherman giant sequoia is nearly 276 ft (84 m) tall – almost 50 times taller than the average man. Even a giraffe would need a ladder to reach its lowest branches.

Average man: 5 ft 9 in (1.75 m)

Giraffe: 19 ft (5.8 m)

Adult golden eagle: 35 in (88 cm) from peak to tail

Egg: 3 in (8 cm)

Chick: 5 in (13 cm)

Kangaroos sure can grow

A newborn kangaroo, or joey, is about the size of a paper clip. By the time it is fully grown it is some 30,000 times heavier than when it was born. The average newborn human baby weighs 7.5 lb (3.4 kg). An adult human 30,000 times heavier than that would weigh 112 tons (102 tonnes) – almost as much as a blue whale.

Joey drawn to scale of mother

Adult kangaroo: 44-66 lb (20-30 kg)

Joey (actual size): 0.026-0.035 oz (0.75-1 g)

Blue whale: 143 tons (130 tonnes)

Adult kangaroo drawn to scale of whale

Adult human drawn to scale of whale

112-ton (102-tonne) adult human

Crocodile outgrows eagle

Golden eagles and Nile crocodiles both hatch from 3-in (8-cm) long eggs. However, a newly hatched Nile crocodile is twice as long as a newly hatched golden eagle, while a fully grown Nile crocodile can be nearly six times as long as a fully grown golden eagle.

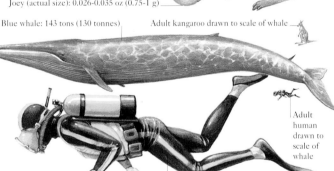

Newly hatched Nile crocodile: 10 in (26 cm)

Egg: 5 in (8 cm)

Adult Nile crocodile: up to 16 ft 5 in (5 m)

Giant tortoise: up to 100 years – maybe even 150

Giant sequoia: up to 4,000 years

Bristlecone pine: more than 5,000 years

Olive tree: 3,000 years or more

Mountain Methuselah

Bristlecone pines can live for more than 5,000 years. The oldest living specimen is on Wheeler Peak, in Nevada. Named Methuselah, after the old man in the Bible, it is thought to be 4,900 years old.

THE HUMAN BODY

THE AMAZING MACHINE that is the human body is full of surprises. Spread out flat, the average adult's skin is large enough to cover 10 copies of this book, front and back, while the air sacs in the lungs of three adults could cover a whole tennis court. Bone can withstand tremendous forces, but is itself incredibly light – when walking, the average adult presses down on each thighbone with the weight of an elephant, yet the whole skeleton accounts for only a sixth of the body's total weight. But perhaps the most remarkable organ in the human body is the brain, which triples in weight between birth and adulthood until it weighs as much as the heart and both lungs put together. In relation to body size, the human brain is larger than the brain of any animal on Earth.

The average adult's thighbones are about 20 in (50 cm) long. This one is drawn actual size.

Grain of rice (actual size)

The average adult's stirrup bones are 0.1 in (3 mm) long – about as big as a grain of rice.

Big bones, little bones

You are born with about 300 bones in your body. As you grow, some of them fuse together – you have about 200 as an adult. The biggest bones, the thighbones, or femurs, are more than 150 times as long as the smallest, the stirrup bones, or stapes, one inside each ear.

Bone can bear the weight

Bone is immensely strong – but then it needs to be. When walking, each step of an adult of average weight exerts a downward pressure on each thighbone of about 12,000 lb per sq in (844 kg per sq cm) – about the weight of a bull African elephant – and the thinnest part of the thighbone is only about 1 in (2.5 cm) thick! When running and jumping, the pressure on the thighbones is even greater.

A bull African elephant weighs about 5.5 tons (5 tonnes).

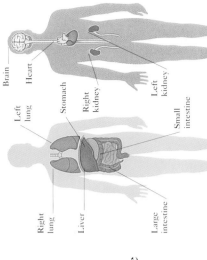

Your body – the inside story

Most of us have only a vague idea of the locations of the main organs inside our bodies. For example, most people think the heart is on the left side of the chest, when in fact it is located centrally, between the lungs.

Brain

Heart

Left lung

Stomach

Right kidney

Left kidney

Right lung

Liver

Small intestine

Large intestine

Long in the tooth

If you have ever been unlucky enough to have had any teeth pulled out, you know that they are much bigger than they look. This is because they have long roots that attach firmly into bony sockets under your gums. But even the largest human teeth are tiny compared with an elephant's massive chomping equipment.

The biggest elephant teeth can weigh as much as 9 lb (4 kg) each, and measure up to 12 in (30 cm) long, including the root – like the one shown here, actual size.

The largest human teeth, molars, grow to up to 1.5 in (4 cm) long. This one is drawn actual size.

When walking, the average adult exerts a pressure on each thighbone equivalent to the weight of a bull African elephant.

Light as bone

Although bone is extremely strong, it is surprisingly light, accounting for only about a sixth of the average adult's overall body weight. Put another way, one person weighs the same as six skeletons – even more if that person is overweight.

The skeleton of the average man weighs only about 24 lb (11 kg).

Thighbone

The average man weighs 141 lb (64 kg) – as much as six skeletons.

20 in (50 cm)

14 in (35 cm)

12 in (30 cm)

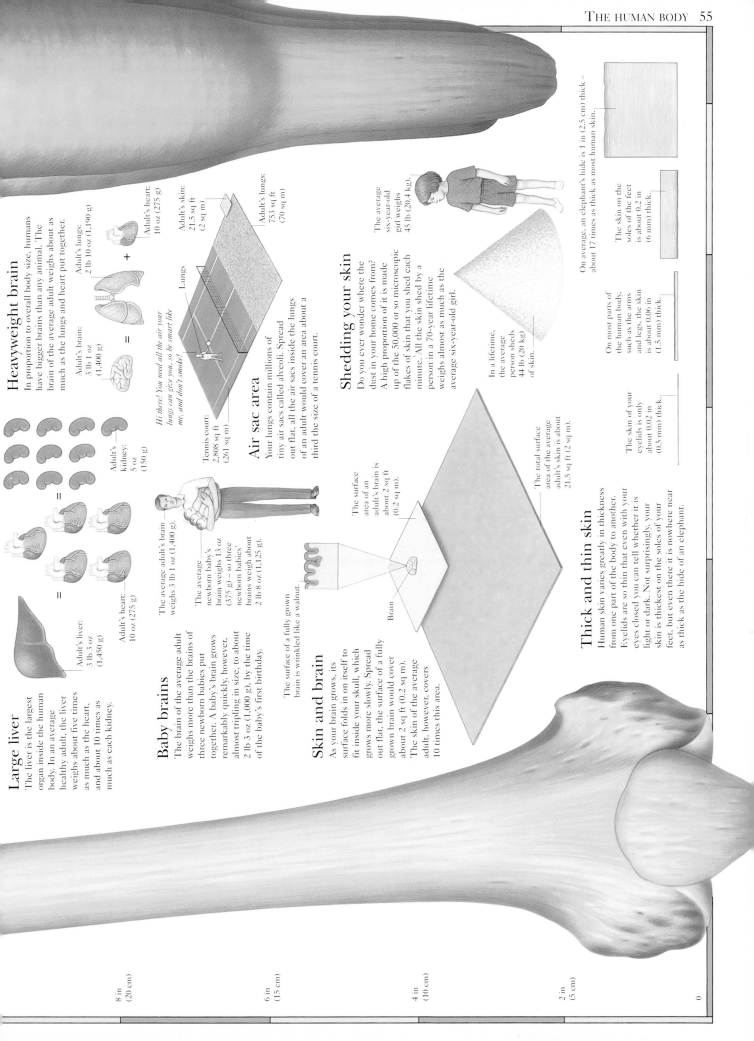

Large liver

The liver is the largest organ inside the human body. In an average healthy adult, the liver weighs about five times as much as the heart, and about 10 times as much as each kidney.

Adult's liver: 3 lb 3 oz (1,450 g)

Adult's heart: 10 oz (275 g)

Adult's kidney: 5 oz (150 g)

Heavyweight brain

In proportion to overall body size, humans have bigger brains than any animal. The brain of the average adult weighs about as much as the lungs and heart put together.

Adult's brain: 3 lb 1 oz (1,400 g)

Adult's lungs: 2 lb 10 oz (1,190 g)

Adult's heart: 10 oz (275 g)

Lungs

Hi there! You need all the air your lungs can give you, so be smart like me, and don't smoke!

Adult's skin: 21.5 sq ft (2 sq m)

Adult's lungs: 753 sq ft (70 sq m)

Air sac area

Your lungs contain millions of tiny air sacs called alveoli. Spread out flat, all the air sacs inside the lungs of an adult would cover an area about a third the size of a tennis court.

Tennis court: 2,808 sq ft (261 sq m)

Baby brains

The brain of the average adult weighs more than the brains of three newborn babies put together. A baby's brain grows remarkably quickly, however, almost tripling in size, to about 2 lb 3 oz (1,000 g), by the time of the baby's first birthday.

The average adult's brain weighs 3 lb 1 oz (1,400 g).

The average newborn baby's brain weighs 13 oz (375 g) – so three newborn babies' brains weigh about 2 lb 8 oz (1,125 g).

Skin and brain

As your brain grows, its surface folds in on itself to fit inside your skull, which grows more slowly. Spread out flat, the surface of a fully grown brain would cover about 2 sq ft (0.2 sq m). The skin of the average adult, however, covers 10 times this area.

The surface of a fully grown brain is wrinkled like a walnut.

Brain

The surface area of an adult's brain is about 2 sq ft (0.2 sq m).

Shedding your skin

Do you ever wonder where the dust in your home comes from? A high proportion of it is made up of the 50,000 or so microscopic flakes of skin that you shed each minute. All the skin you shed by a person in a 70-year lifetime weighs almost as much as the average six-year-old girl.

The average six-year-old girl weighs 45 lb (20.4 kg).

In a lifetime, the average person sheds 44 lb (20 kg) of skin.

The total surface area of the average adult's skin is about 21.5 sq ft (2 sq m).

Thick and thin skin

Human skin varies greatly in thickness from one part of the body to another. Eyelids are so thin that even with your eyes closed you can tell whether it is light or dark. Not surprisingly, your skin is thickest on the soles of your feet, but even there it is nowhere near as thick as the hide of an elephant.

The skin of your eyelids is only about 0.02 in (0.5 mm) thick.

On most parts of the human body, such as the arms and legs, the skin is about 0.06 in (1.5 mm) thick.

On average, an elephant's hide is 1 in (2.5 cm) thick – about 17 times as thick as most human skin.

The skin on the soles of the feet is about 0.2 in (6 mm) thick.

8 in (20 cm)

6 in (15 cm)

4 in (10 cm)

2 in (5 cm)

0

THE BODY AT WORK

ADVANCES IN MEDICAL SCIENCE mean that many of us can now expect to enjoy long, relatively healthy lives of 70 years or more. But nothing in medical science can match the natural miracle that sees us grow from a dot-size fertilized egg into a fully developed baby in the space of just 40 weeks. We are born with all our organs in full working order, and for most of us they will last, largely unaided, until our dying day. By then, they will have performed some incredible feats. Our lungs will have inhaled and exhaled enough air to fill either of the two largest airships ever built – one-and-a-half times over. Our hearts will have beaten more than 2,500,000,000 times – pumping enough blood around the body to fill the fuel tanks of 700 jumbo jets in the process. And our stomachs and intestines will have digested the weight of six bull African elephants or more in food!

Every breath you take

When you do something strenuous, such as swimming or running, you breathe deeply and rapidly. At rest, you take shallower, less frequent breaths. When breathing normally, however, you take in about 30.5 cubic in (500 cubic cm) of air with each breath, at an average rate of 15 breaths a minute. Based on normal breathing, in a 70-year lifetime you will breathe about 9,711,543 cubic ft (275,000 cubic m) of air – enough to fill either of the two largest airships ever built almost one-and-a-half times over.

Every beat of your heart

Your heart is an amazingly strong and hard-wearing muscle. On average, it beats 70 times a minute, and pumps 3.6 cubic in (59 cubic cm) of blood with each beat. In a 70-year lifetime, that works out to more than 2,500,000,000 beats, pumping about 40,154,144 gallons (152,000,000 liters) of blood – enough to fill the fuel tanks of 10 Boeing 747 jumbo jets every year.

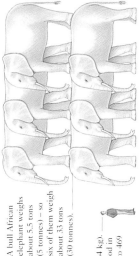

A bull African elephant weighs about 5.5 tons (5 tonnes) – so six of them weigh about 33 tons (30 tonnes).

Elephantine appetites

The amount of food that people eat varies from person to person and from country to country, but in a 70-year lifetime the average person in a rich country such as the US eats an estimated 33 tons (30 tonnes) of food – the weight of six bull African elephants.

The average man weighs 141 lb (64 kg). If he eats 33 tons (30 tonnes) of food in a 70-year lifetime, that works out to 469 times his adult body weight.

Like her sister ship *Hindenburg*, the 1930s airship *Graf Zeppelin II* was 804 ft (245 m) long, and held about 7,062,940 cubic ft (200,000 cubic m) of hydrogen. In a 70-year lifetime, the average person breathes enough air to fill *Graf Zeppelin II* almost one-and-a-half times over.

Hi! I think I'll stick to blowing up balloons in the future!

Your heart beats faster when you exercise, and slower when you rest, but on average it beats 70 times a minute.

When full, the fuel tanks of a jumbo jet hold 57,325 gallons (217,000 liters).

Vast area of vessels

As well as larger veins and arteries, your body contains millions of tiny blood vessels called capillaries. Minute tubes, each slightly more than 0.04 in (1 mm) long, they carry blood to all parts of your body. All the capillaries in the average adult's body form a huge network that, if spread out flat, would cover about 53,821 sq ft (5,000 sq m) – an area greater than that covered by 19 tennis courts.

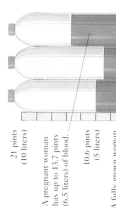

All the capillaries in the average adult's body could cover an area greater than 19 tennis courts.

Fist-size filters

You have two kidneys, each about the size of a clenched fist. They filter waste products and excess water from your blood, then pass these on to your bladder in the form of urine. Although the kidneys of the average adult filter about 2.5 pints (1.2 liters) of blood every minute of the day, they only extract about 3 pints (1.4 liters) of urine each day.

21 pints (10 liters)

10.6 pints (5 liters)

4 pints (2 liters)

2 pints (1 liter)

0

A pregnant woman has up to 13.7 pints (6.5 liters) of blood.

A fully grown woman has about 9.5 pints (4.5 liters) of blood.

A fully grown man has about 10.6 pints (5 liters) of blood.

The kidneys of the average adult weigh about 5 oz (150 g) each, and are about the size of a clenched fist.

Every minute, the kidneys of the average adult filter about 2.5 pints (1.2 liters) of blood.

Each day, the kidneys of the average adult extract about 3 pints (1.4 liters) of urine from the blood.

The blood in your body

Blood might be thicker than water, but even a few drops of it can spread over a surprisingly large area – as you know if you have ever cut yourself badly. Being generally smaller, women usually have less blood than men. When pregnant, however, a woman produces extra blood to supply her growing baby.

From fertilized egg to full-size fetus

Before you are even born, your body undergoes a phenomenal increase in size. You begin life as a fertilized egg no bigger than the period that ends this sentence. After four weeks of rapid growth you are about as big as a pea – at this stage you are called an embryo. After eight weeks you are about the size of a brazil nut – from then on you are called a fetus. Finally, after 40 weeks, you are fully developed and, curled up inside your mother's womb, are about the size of a football.

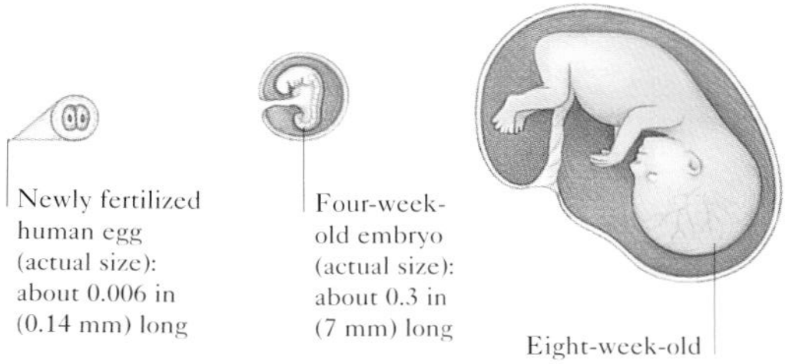

Nineteen tennis courts cover an area of 53,380 sq ft (4,959 sq m).

Adult drawn to scale of tennis courts

Curled up in the womb, a 40-week-old fetus is about as big as a football.

Size for size, a baby's head is twice as big as an adult's. A baby's head is about a quarter of the length of its body, an adult's about an eighth.

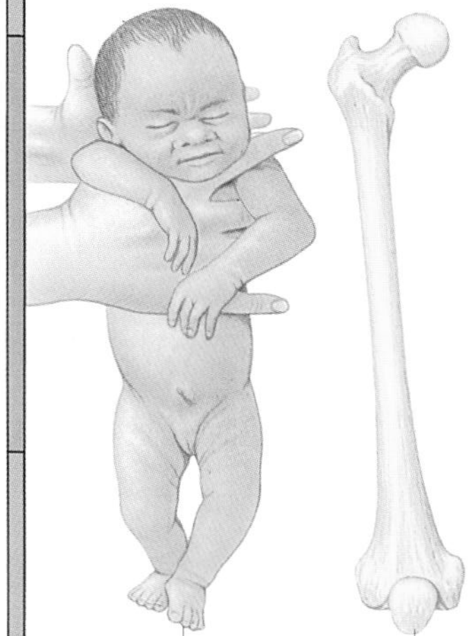

Newly fertilized human egg (actual size): about 0.006 in (0.14 mm) long

Four-week-old embryo (actual size): about 0.3 in (7 mm) long

Eight-week-old fetus (actual size): about 1.2 in (3 cm) long

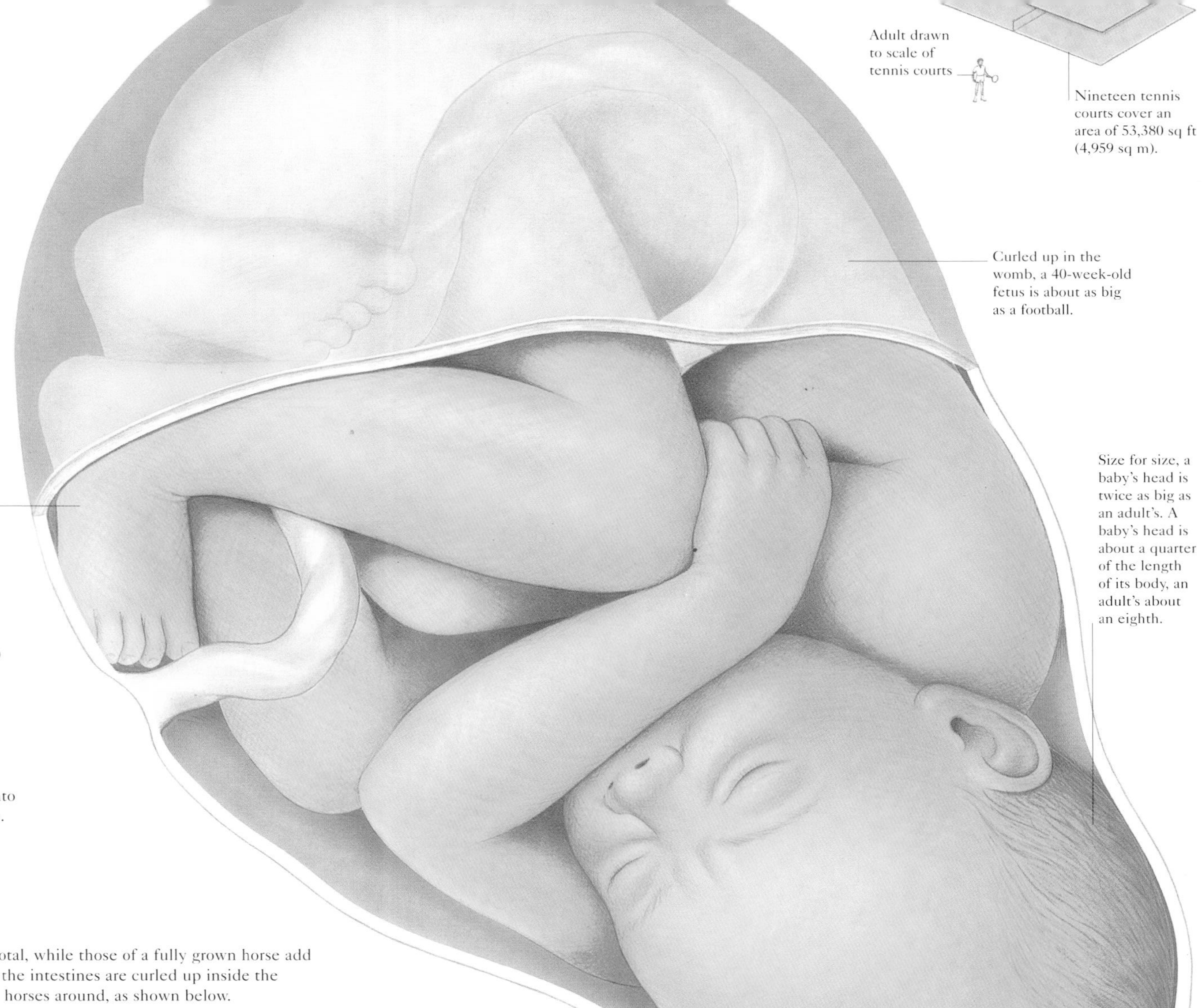

Forty-week-old fetus (actual size): about 20 in (50 cm) long

Bone-size baby

The average newborn baby measures about 20 in (50 cm) from head to toe, which is about the same height as the average adult's thighbone. Although you grow rapidly inside your mother's body, it takes you about 18 years to grow from a newborn baby into a full-size adult (see page 53).

Adult's thighbone: 20 in (50 cm)

Newborn baby: 20 in (50 cm)

Straight from the horse's mouth?

Stretched out, an adult's intestines are about 25 ft (7.5 m) long in total, while those of a fully grown horse add up to an amazing 89 ft (27 m) – almost four times as long. Luckily, the intestines are curled up inside the body, otherwise there would be some very odd-looking people and horses around, as shown below.

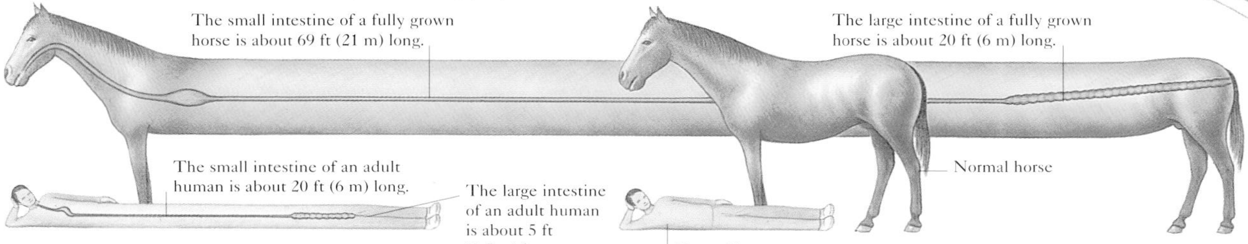

The small intestine of a fully grown horse is about 69 ft (21 m) long.

The large intestine of a fully grown horse is about 20 ft (6 m) long.

Normal horse

The small intestine of an adult human is about 20 ft (6 m) long.

The large intestine of an adult human is about 5 ft (1.5 m) long.

Normal human

The 0.06-in (1.5-mm) common flea can jump almost 8 in (20 cm) high – equivalent to a 5-ft 9-in (1.75-m) man jumping 746 ft (227.5 m).

HUMANS AND ANIMALS

ARE HUMANS SUPERIOR to animals? When it comes to brain power, we like to think that we are well ahead of even the most intelligent animals, such as dolphins. Two things with which we identify our superiority are our use of tools, and our ability to talk. Plainly, however, plenty of creatures are much stronger than we are – no human could ever beat a gorilla in a wrestling match. Nor are we necessarily physically superior to creatures that are much smaller than we are. Size for size, ants are even stronger than gorillas. We cannot survive in many of the environments animals can, either. Birds fly at altitudes where we would be unable to breathe, and sperm whales can swim at depths where the water pressure would quickly kill us. Only with the aid of machines can we safely venture into the worlds of these animals.

Tail feathers top hair

There are several recorded examples of women who have been able to grow their hair to more than twice their height. This achievement falls well short of the remarkable Japanese Phoenix fowl, however, which has been selectively bred over the years to grow longer and longer tail feathers – up to lengths almost twice as long as a giraffe is tall.

Human hair grows about 0.5 in (1.2 cm) a month. Uncut, it usually stops growing when it is 2-3 ft (60-90 cm) long. But some women are able to grow their hair to nearly 13 ft (4 m).

The longest recorded tail feathers on a Japanese Phoenix fowl were an amazing 34 ft 9 in (10.6 m).

The giraffe is the tallest animal in the world, growing up to 19 ft (5.8 m) in height.

The mighty ant

A human can squash an ant under a fingertip, but, size for size, ants are much stronger than we are. An ant can lift and carry about 50 times its own body weight. This is equivalent to a 141-lb (64-kg) man lifting 7,055 lb (3,200 kg) – about the weight of three cars.

If humans were as strong as ants, a 141-lb (64-kg) man would be able to lift three cars over his head.

Muscle-bound gorillas

Gorillas are up to eight times stronger than humans. If gorillas lifted weights, the world weightlifting record might be increased from 586 lb (266 kg) to 4,691 lb (2,128 kg).

In 1988, Leonid Taranenko, of the then Soviet Union, set a new world weightlifting record for men of 586 lb (266 kg) – equivalent to lifting four 141-lb (64-kg) men above his head.

In 1992, Li Yajuan, of China, set a new world weightlifting record for women of 331 lb (150 kg).

If gorillas lifted weights, they might be able to lift more than 2 tons (2 tonnes) – about the weight of two cars.

Enjoying the high life

Although many mountaineers have climbed the highest mountain in the world, Mt. Everest, without special breathing equipment, humans are only able to ascend to greater heights in aircraft and balloons with the aid of oxygen. Some birds, however, appear to be able to fly at almost one-and-a-half times the height of Everest without difficulty. But the really high fliers are airborne bacteria, which have been found at almost five times the height of Everest.

Airborne bacteria have been found alive and well at a height of 134,514 ft (41,000 m).

Deep beneath the waves

Most humans cannot hold their breath underwater for more than a few seconds. Scuba divers cannot safely dive much below about 164 ft (50 m) because of the dangerous effects on the body of high water pressure. But some sea animals have no such problems. Sperm whales hunting giant squid might dive six times as deep as the Empire State Building is tall – holding their breath underwater for hours at a time.

Migrating whooper swans sometimes fly at more than 27,000 ft (8,230 m). But the record for high flying goes to the Rüppell's griffon, a kind of vulture. In 1973, above the Ivory Coast, a Rüppell's griffon collided with an aircraft at 37,000 ft (11,278 m).

Mt. Everest, in the Himalayas, is 29,028 ft (8,848 m) high. It was first climbed in 1953 by Edmund Hillary and Sherpa Tenzing.

Toads live at up to 26,247 ft (8,000 m) in the Himalayas.

Jumping spiders have been found living at 22,000 ft (6,706 m) on Mt. Everest.

Yaks are frequently seen at 19,685 ft (6,000 m) or more in the Himalayas.

39,370 ft (12,000 m)

36,089 ft (11,000 m)

32,808 ft (10,000 m)

29,528 ft (9,000 m)

26,247 ft (8,000 m)

22,966 ft (7,000 m)

19,685 ft (6,000 m)

16,404 ft (5,000 m)

9,843 ft (3,000 m)
6,562 ft (2,000 m)
3,281 ft (1,000 m)
0
3,281 ft (1,000 m)
6,562 ft (2,000 m)
9,843 ft (3,000 m)
13,123 ft (4,000 m)
16,404 ft (5,000 m)
19,685 ft (6,000 m)
22,966 ft (7,000 m)
26,247 ft (8,000 m)
29,528 ft (9,000 m)
32,808 ft (10,000 m)

Hi there, landlubbers! I can hold my breath for two minutes or more, but only because I have trained for years, so don't try this at home!

Holding their breath, pearl divers can descend 49 ft (15 m), and sponge divers twice this depth.

Antarctic Emperor penguins can dive to 869 ft (265 m).

Sperm whales regularly dive to 3,937 ft (1,200 m), and possibly to 7,874 ft (2,400 m) or more at times — a depth more than six times the height of New York's Empire State Building.

Some brotulid fish live 27,231 ft (8,300 m) deep in the sea.

Shrimplike amphipods live at 34,449 ft (10,500 m) in the depths of the Pacific Ocean.

Sea urchins live near the bottom of the Marianas Trench, in the Pacific Ocean, at 35,138 ft (10,710 m).

Sleep comes first

On average, humans need eight hours of sleep a day. The amount of sleep that animals need varies enormously. Shrews never sleep, except when hibernating, while koalas are seldom awake. Between these extremes, cats like nothing better than to curl up in front of a warm fire. The clocks show the average length of time each animal sleeps in a day.

12:00 — Gorilla
08:00 — Human
03:54 — Asian elephant
03:48 — Sheep
00:00 — Shrew

22:00 — Koala
20:00 — Sloth
18:06 — Giant armadillo
14:30 — Cat
13:00 — Pig

High achievers

Top high jumpers can leap almost as high as the Australian red kangaroo — yet are leaden-footed compared with some animals. While we struggle to jump above head-high — even with a run-up — the klipspringer antelope of southern Africa can jump 15 times its height. But fleas are the stars — from rest, a common flea can hop as high as 130 times its body size.

The 20-in (50-cm) tall klipspringer can jump 25 ft (7.5 m) high — equivalent to a 5-ft 9-in (1.75-m) man jumping 86 ft (26.25 m).

Leaps and bounds

Like top high jumpers, top long jumpers can almost match the red kangaroo — with a fast run-up. But several much smaller animals can jump much farther in relation to their size — and from a standing start. As in the high jump, fleas are the champions.

In 1991, Mike Powell, of the U.S, set a new world long jump record for men with a leap of 29 ft 4.5 in (8.95 m).

Red kangaroos can cover 30 ft (9 m) or more in one bound.

The 6.5-ft (2-m) tall red kangaroo can spring 10 ft (3 m) into the air.

In 1989, Javier Sotomayor, of Cuba, set a new world high jump record for men by clearing 8 ft 0.5 in (2.45 m).

Bulgarian Stefka Kostadinova set a world women's high jump record of 6 ft 10.25 in (2.09 m) in 1987.

A 12-in (30-cm) long goliath frog can jump 10 ft (3 m) — 10 times its body length.

A 5-ft 9-in (1.75-m) man jumping 10 times his body length would cover 57 ft (17.5 m).

A 10-in (25-cm) long Asian grasshopper can jump 15 ft (4.5 m) – 18 body lengths.

A 5-ft 9-in (1.75-m) man jumping 18 times his body length would cover 103 ft (31.5 m).

A 4-in (10-cm) long jerboa, or desert rat, can jump 15 ft (4.5 m) — 45 times its body length.

A 5-ft 9-in (1.75-m) man jumping 45 times his body length would cover 258 ft (78.75 m).

Fleas jump the farthest

The amazing jumping abilities of *Palex irritans*, the common flea, were measured in a series of experiments conducted by M. B. Mitzmain, a US scientist, in 1910.

A 0.06-in (1.5-mm) common flea can jump up to 13 in (33 cm) lengthwise – 220 times its body size.

A 5-ft 9-in (1.75-m) man jumping 220 times his body length would cover 1,263 ft (385 m).

66 ft (20 m)
33 ft (10 m)
0

131 ft (40 m)
98 ft (30 m)
66 ft (20 m)
33 ft (10 m)
0

262 ft (80 m)
197 ft (60 m)
131 ft (40 m)
66 ft (20 m)
0

13 in (33 cm)
0

1,312 ft (400 m)
984 ft (300 m)
656 ft (200 m)
328 ft (100 m)
0

PART TWO
THE WORLD IN ONE DAY

A DAY AROUND THE WORLD

WHAT HAPPENS IN ONE DAY in the life of the world? In the next 24 hours, the world will spin once on its axis and travel more than 1.5 million miles (2.5 million km) in its orbit around the Sun. As they hurtle through space, 2.5 billion people will spend the day at work, and 1 billion children will go to school. But what else is going on? This section gives you the figures for many of the other things that happen in an average day, from how much water an elephant drinks and how many times a flea can jump, to how many potatoes are harvested and how much gold is made into false teeth. So fasten your seat belt as we lift off into the bizarre world of real facts. Enjoy it, and remember . . . tomorrow is another day.

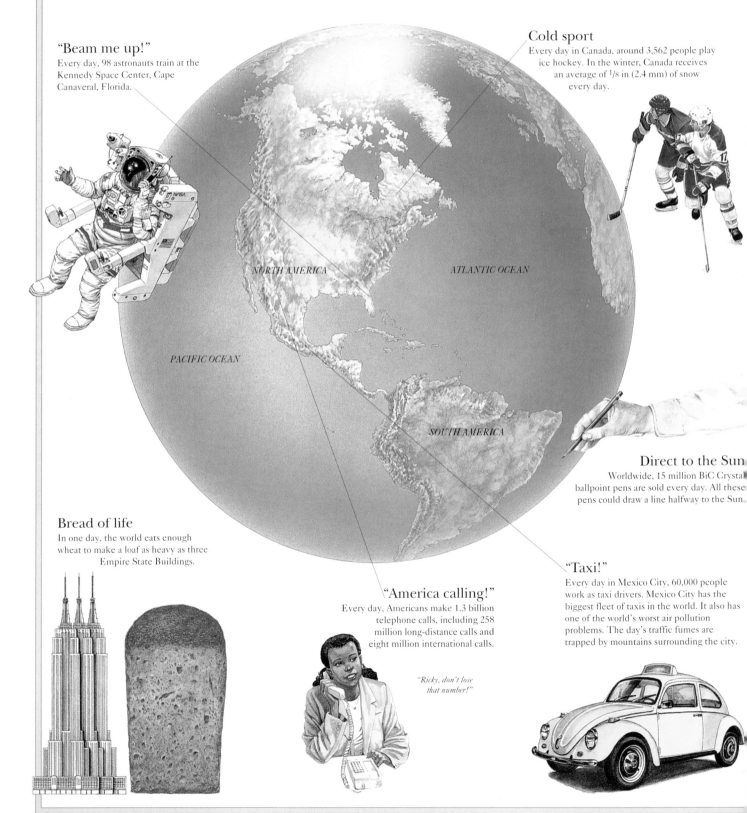

"Beam me up!"
Every day, 98 astronauts train at the Kennedy Space Center, Cape Canaveral, Florida.

Cold sport
Every day in Canada, around 3,562 people play ice hockey. In the winter, Canada receives an average of 1/8 in (2.4 mm) of snow every day.

NORTH AMERICA

ATLANTIC OCEAN

PACIFIC OCEAN

SOUTH AMERICA

Direct to the Sun
Worldwide, 15 million BiC Crystal ballpoint pens are sold every day. All these pens could draw a line halfway to the Sun.

Bread of life
In one day, the world eats enough wheat to make a loaf as heavy as three Empire State Buildings.

"America calling!"
Every day, Americans make 1.3 billion telephone calls, including 258 million long-distance calls and eight million international calls.

"Ricky, don't lose that number!"

"Taxi!"
Every day in Mexico City, 60,000 people work as taxi drivers. Mexico City has the biggest fleet of taxis in the world. It also has one of the world's worst air pollution problems. The day's traffic fumes are trapped by mountains surrounding the city.

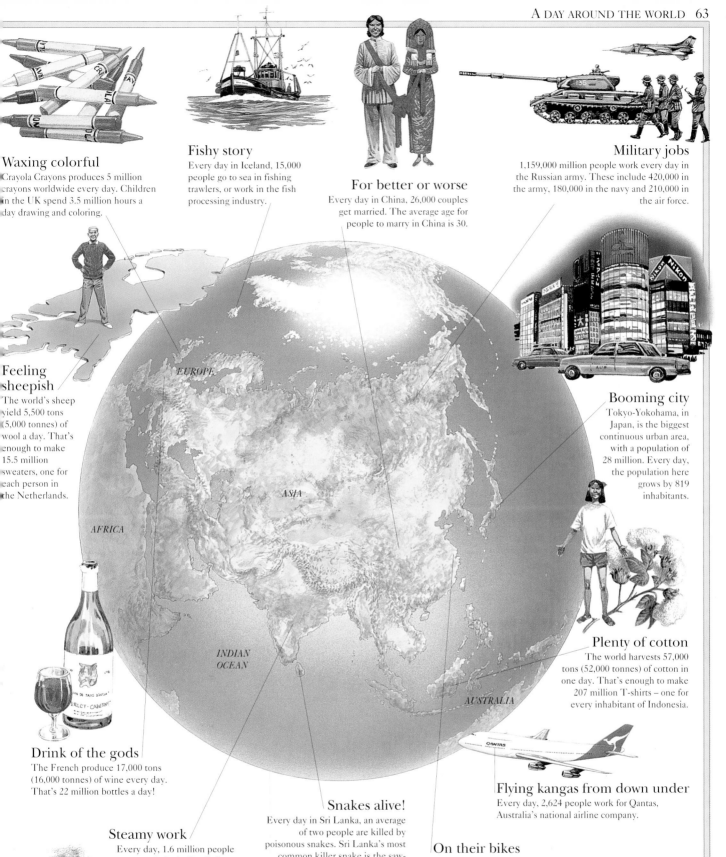

Waxing colorful
Crayola Crayons produces 5 million crayons worldwide every day. Children in the UK spend 3.5 million hours a day drawing and coloring.

Fishy story
Every day in Iceland, 15,000 people go to sea in fishing trawlers, or work in the fish processing industry.

For better or worse
Every day in China, 26,000 couples get married. The average age for people to marry in China is 30.

Military jobs
1,159,000 million people work every day in the Russian army. These include 420,000 in the army, 180,000 in the navy and 210,000 in the air force.

Feeling sheepish
The world's sheep yield 5,500 tons (5,000 tonnes) of wool a day. That's enough to make 15.5 million sweaters, one for each person in the Netherlands.

EUROPE

AFRICA

ASIA

Booming city
Tokyo-Yokohama, in Japan, is the biggest continuous urban area, with a population of 28 million. Every day, the population here grows by 819 inhabitants.

INDIAN
OCEAN

Plenty of cotton
The world harvests 57,000 tons (52,000 tonnes) of cotton in one day. That's enough to make 207 million T-shirts – one for every inhabitant of Indonesia.

AUSTRALIA

Drink of the gods
The French produce 17,000 tons (16,000 tonnes) of wine every day. That's 22 million bottles a day!

Flying kangas from down under
Every day, 2,624 people work for Qantas, Australia's national airline company.

Steamy work
Every day, 1.6 million people go to work for Indian Railways, the biggest nongovernmental employer in the world.

Snakes alive!
Every day in Sri Lanka, an average of two people are killed by poisonous snakes. Sri Lanka's most common killer snake is the saw-scaled or carpet viper, one of the most poisonous snakes in the world.

On their bikes
The people of Shanghai, in China, make 2.5 million bicycle trips every day. Shanghai also has the world's largest bicycle manufacturer, the Forever Bicycle Factory, which makes 4,500 bikes every day.

PLANET EARTH

SINCE IT CAME INTO BEING ABOUT 4.6 billion years ago, Earth has continued to evolve every day. Heat from the Earth's core forces molten material to bubble to the surface in volcanoes. The plates that form the hard outer layers of the Earth grind against one another. The enormous pressure they exert pushes mountain ranges gradually higher, pulls the continents apart, and causes tremors and earthquakes. Wind, ice, and water wear away at rock. Earth's landscape is steadily changing day by day.

Volcanic energy

The energy released in one day by the eruption of Mount Tambora was thought to be 16,000 megatons – making it 800,000 times as powerful as the Hiroshima atom bomb.

Great balls of fire

Mount Vesuvius erupted in AD 79. Lava exploded into the air as ash and buried Pompeii. Its inhabitants were asphyxiated by poisonous gases. Ash then mixed with rain to create hot mud flows (lahars), which buried Herculaneum in just one day. The lethal lahars would have kept up with a modern Italian trying to escape on a moped.

"I'm burning rubber! Hey! Get this lahar off my tail!"

Earth in orbit

Planet Earth spins so fast on its axis that a person standing on the Equator is actually traveling at 1,038 mph (1,670 kmh) – the speed of the Concorde – without moving at all.

In a flash

Lightning strikes somewhere on Earth 100 times a second. A lot of it zigzags straight into the sea or hits icecaps or huge uninhabited areas of land, so the chances of getting struck by lightning are quite remote. The odds are higher in the tropics, where 3,200 electric storms rend the air every 12 night hours.

Powering Nicaragua by tropical storms

Lightning power

If the power of all the tropical storms that take place in 24 hours could be harnessed, it would be equal to a full year's electricity consumption in a small country like Nicaragua.

Nightly fireworks

Stromboli is a volcano that has been active every day for thousands of years. The ancients called it the Lighthouse of the Mediterranean because it produces a spectacular display of sizzling bombs and red fountains of lava against the night sky.

Mount Stromboli could go on erupting for hundreds of years before it becomes dormant and finally extinct.

The Bering Glacier in the Arctic began to retreat in the 1980s, raising fears about global warming. In 1993 it started to advance again.

The ice advances

Most glaciers are slow movers. They grind forward by about 6 ft (2 m) a day. The Bering Glacier in the Arctic is an exception. It advances an astonishing 300 ft (91 m) every day. It could transform a large backyard into a skating rink overnight.

Jupiter	Saturn	Neptune	Uranus	Earth	Mars	Pluto	Mercury	Venus
9h 55m	10h 39m	16h 7m	17h 14m	24h	24h 37m	6 days 9h	58 days 14h	244 days

How long is a day?

A day on Earth lasts 24 hours, but a day on Venus lasts eight Earth months, because Venus spins so slowly. Jupiter spins so fast that a day flashes by in under 10 hours. An Earth watch would have to lose 2 minutes an hour to keep time on the Moon.

Cosmic dust

Every day 121 tons of cosmic dust – debris from outer space – enters Earth's atmosphere. If it could all be shoveled into one heap, it would be as big as a two-story house.

America by storm
In one day, a hurricane could produce enough energy to replace the whole of the US's electricity supply for nine months.

Powering the US by hurricane

A day's work for the Sun
Every day the Sun beams 4 trillion kilowatt hours of energy to Earth. This recycles Earth's water by evaporation, causes winds, waves, and ocean currents, and is used in photosynthesis.

Squeaky clean
Enough rain falls to Earth every day for each one of its inhabitants to have a bath every five minutes.

Wet, wet, wet
If all the moisture in Earth's atmosphere fell as rain, it would produce 300 cu miles (1,250 cu km) of water. If all this rain fell in one day on the island of Manhattan, it would submerge it to a depth of 3.7 miles (22 km).

SMALL WORLD
Biosphere 2 is a huge greenhouse built in Arizona. Inside the Biosphere are areas of farmland, rain forest, desert, and even an ocean. This is the home of an experiment in global warming. Levels of carbon dioxide (CO_2) in Earth's atmosphere are rising. Scientists will steadily pump more CO_2 into the Biosphere in order to predict Earth's future.

Solar energy
It would take 167,000 nuclear power stations to produce the amount of energy that the Sun beams down to Earth in one day.

When the wind blows
Erosion is the wearing away and removal of land surfaces by running water, wind, or ice. Erosion is greatest in sloping areas and areas of little or no surface vegetation. On the west coast of Mauritania near Nouakchott, prevailing easterly winds carry 767,000 tons of sand and dust from the Sahara Desert into the Atlantic Ocean every day.

Cold snout
The end of a glacier is called the snout. At the snout, the ice either melts as fast as it arrives, or the glacier calves – bits break off to form icebergs. Jakobshavn Glacier in Greenland discharges 20 to 30 million tons of ice a day to the fjord at its snout.

Sand from the Sahara blows into the Atlantic from the west coast of Africa.

Icebergs calve at the snout of Jakobshavn Glacier in Greenland.

A raging torrent
The Iguaçu Falls are a string of 275 waterfalls on the border between Argentina and Brazil, close to Paraguay. The water of the Iguaçu River cascades down spectacular drops of up to 230 ft (70 m). At times of peak flow, enough water passes over the Falls to fill six Olympic swimming pools every second. However, in some years rainfall is so light that this great river can dry up completely, as it did in 1978.

The Earth moves
An earthquake happens when rocks move along faults. Earthquakes are especially powerful when the tectonic plates that form the Earth's outer layers move against one another. The Great African Rift Valley in Djibouti experiences dozens of earthquakes every day, indicating the continuous movement of the tectonic plates beneath Africa.

A DAY TO REMEMBER

Up to your ears
The wettest day ever was March 15, 1952, when 74 in (190 cm) of torrential rain fell at Cilaos on the island of La Réunion in the Indian Ocean.

Taking a beating
On July 14, 1953, golf ball-sized hailstones fell in a freak storm in Alberta, Canada. Powered by gale-force winds, they bashed to death 36,000 ducks.

Buried
The biggest snowfall ever was recorded on February 7, 1963, when 78 in (198 cm) of snow fell at Mile 47 Camp, Cooper River Division, Alaska.

Sunny side up
On September 13, 1922, the temperature in the shade at al'Aziziyah in the Libyan desert reached 136°F (57.8°C) – hot enough to fry an egg on a rock.

PLANTS

WITHOUT PLANTS, THERE WOULD BE no animal life on Earth. Plants produce oxygen, which all creatures need to breathe and to convert food into energy. Their fruits, leaves, and seeds give us food and medicines. Their fibers are woven into clothes. Their juices give us drinks and dyes. Trunks and branches provide shelter, fuel, and material for furniture and tools. So far, we have identified 500,000 plants, and still more await discovery. Yet large areas of natural vegetation are disappearing. Every day, 89,000 acres (36,000 hectares) of tropical rain forest are destroyed. But just one Amazonian Brazil nut tree can produce more nutritious food than can be cultivated on the land that is cleared when the tree is felled.

Plant growth

Plants harness energy from the Sun's rays, turning it into glucose, which they use to grow. This process is called photosynthesis. A large rain forest tree can produce 3 lb (1.5 kg) of pure glucose in one day, using just sunlight and water. Some plants, like those on the left, grow very quickly. Compared with these plants, even the fastest trees seem to grow slowly. Some of the slowest growing plants are lichens (see bottom right), which can take a century to grow just 1 in (2.5 cm).

Morning glory

Morning glory flowers last only one day. They open in the morning and shrivel and die toward evening. Plants flower by responding to the number of hours of daylight in a day. A light-sensitive pigment in the leaves sends a hormone signal to the flower buds, triggering them to open.

Giant bamboo

A native of Burma, the giant bamboo can grow an astonishing 18 in (46 cm) a day. Bamboo is technically a grass. Its stems are used for making buckets, rafts, and chopsticks. In India and Southeast Asia, the bamboo harvest is turned into 5,291 tons of paper a day.

Giant kelp

Giant kelp is a huge seaweed found in the coastal waters of California. It grows up to 18 in (45 cm) per day. Fronds of kelp form underwater forests, and can reach 328 ft (100 m), making it the tallest plant in the world.

Callie grass

Callie grass grows 6 in (15 cm) in one day.

Titan arum

The center of the titan arum shoots up 3 in (7.5 cm) in a day. Its flowers last just one day, giving off a stench of rotting flesh. In its native Sumatra, the titan arum is known as the "corpse flower."

Eucalyptus deglupta

This eucalyptus is the world's fastest growing tree. It can spurt 1 in (2.5 cm) in a day. One specimen in New Zealand reached 35 ft (10.6 m) in 15 months.

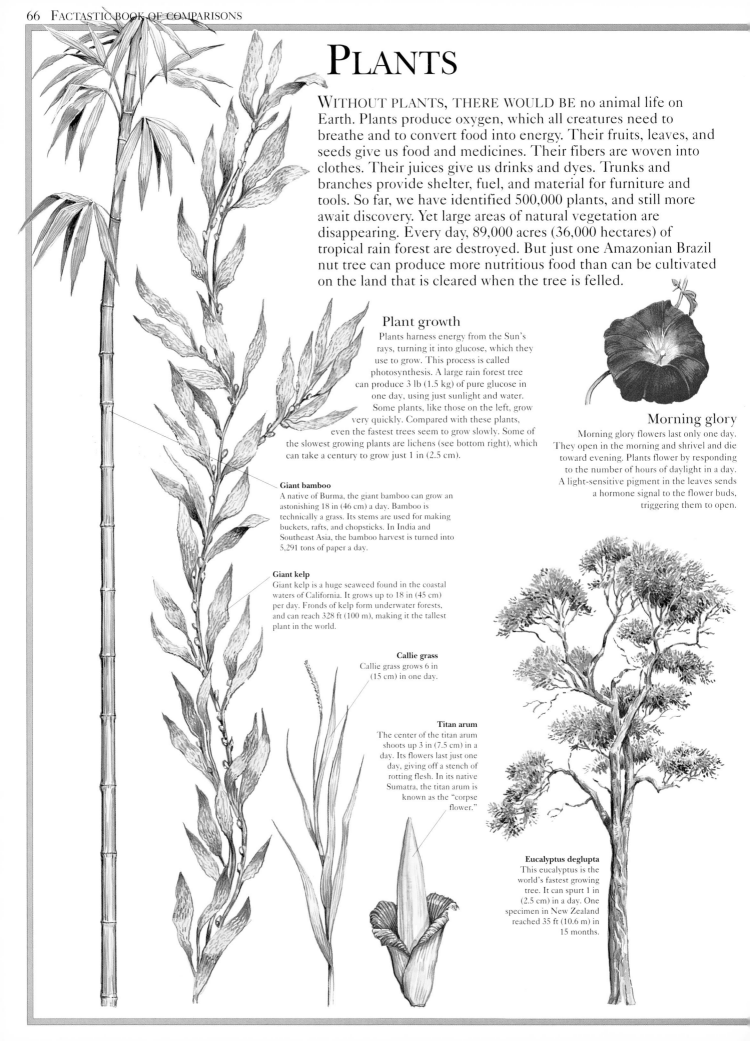

SMALL WORLD

The Royal Botanic Gardens at Kew, near London, UK, house 40,000 living plants, including a growing example of one in 8 of all known flowers, and over 6 million dried plants (9 out of 10 of all species). This is the largest collection of plants in the world. Many of the plants grow in one of several greenhouses at Kew. The greenhouses re-create the conditions of different climates from around the world, ranging from hot desert to cold alpine. Many visitors to Kew feel like they have traveled the globe in just one day.

Giant puffball

The giant puffball fungus can measure up to 6.6 ft (2m) in circumference, and weigh up to 44 lb (20 kg). If an animal or a raindrop strikes the fungus, spores (seeds) are puffed out of a hole in the top. In just one day, a giant puffball can release seven billion spores.

Fairy ring

Toadstools spring from underground filaments called a mycelium. Some toadstools appear as if by magic, in a circle overnight, as the mycelium grows out from a central point. These formations are often called "fairy rings."

Petroleum nut

The petroleum nut tree, which grows in Borneo and the Philippines, produces a high-octane oil in its seeds. The seeds of one tree yield 12 gallons (53 liters) a year, which is about 3 teaspoonful every day. The oil is burned in lamps, and was used by the Japanese during World War II to fuel tanks.

Diesel tree

The copaiba tree, which grows in the Amazon, contains an oil similar to diesel. It can produce 2 gallons (9 liters) of this oil every hour. So one tree could yield 48 gallons (218 liters) of fuel in one day, enough to fill the gas tanks of 5 cars. Diesel trees are now being cultivated in Japan for their oil.

Petroleum plant
Petroleum seed

Rubber tree

When a cut is made in the bark of a rubber tree, a sticky white liquid called latex oozes out. Rubber trees flourish in the warm, moist climates of Malaysia, Indonesia, and Thailand. They produce 18,000 tons of rubber every day.

Oak

Oak trees live to a great age – one in Switzerland is thought to be around 930 years old. A mature oak tree draws 20 gallons (90 liters) of water out of the earth every day. Oak trees are very slow-growing. They only grow 0.055 in (1.4 mm) a day.

Rampant growth

Tropical rain forest grows twice as fast as temperate oakwood. Every acre of warm, wet rain forest produces 165 lb of lush new growth per day (67 lb per acre). Every 2.5 acres of rain forest contains 330 tons of 180 different species of trees, 1.1 tons of plants, 1.1 tons of earthworms, and 18 lb (8 kg) of birds.

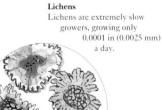

Trumpet tree
Saplings of the trumpet tree growing on the rain forest floor shoot up toward the light at a rate of 0.28 in (7 mm) in one day.

Tasmanian cider gum
One of the fastest-growing of all trees, the cider gum (native to Tasmania) can grow 0.16 in (4 mm) every day.

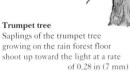

Poplar
A poplar tree grows just over 0.118 in (3 mm) every day.

Bristlecone pine
The bristlecone pine grows very slowly, at a rate of only 0.00035 in (0.009 mm) a day. This tree is very long-lived. One specimen is believed to be 4,600 years old.

Lichens
Lichens are extremely slow growers, growing only 0.0001 in (0.0025 mm) a day.

THE HUMAN BODY

EVERY DAY THE HUMAN BODY needs refueling with oxygen, food, and water. The body's powerhouse is the brain. It accounts for only 2 percent of body weight, but uses 20 percent of our oxygen intake, 20 percent of our calorie intake, and 15 percent of the body's blood supply. To fight disease, each body produces 10 billion new white blood cells a day. Skin cells last for 25 days, red blood cells survive for 120 days, liver cells for 500 days, and some nerve cells last a whole lifetime. The continual process of cell renewal that keeps the body alive is called metabolism.

Body factory

The digestive system, lungs, and kidneys are at work around the clock. The digestive system breaks food into particles so tiny that blood can take nourishment to all parts of the body. The body's entire blood supply passes through the lungs almost once a minute, collecting and distributing oxygen. Waste products are removed from the blood in the kidneys, each of which contains around one million tiny filters called nephrons.

Breathtaking stuff

Each one of us takes around 30,000 breaths a day. If you expelled all the air you breathed in a day into rubber dinghies, you would be able to inflate 50 two-man dinghies in 24 hours.

Bloodbath

The average human heart beats 100,800 times a day. The amount of blood that passes through the heart each day would fill 170 bathtubs.

House of skin

We shed approximately one million dead skin cells every 40 minutes. One person will shed enough skin in a lifetime to fill a suitcase. All the skin shed by the world's people in one day would fill a four-story house.

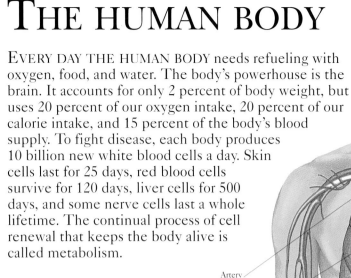

Artery

Lungs

Stomach

Large intestine

Small intestine

Body heat

The total body heat produced in one day by a human being is enough to power a lightbulb for a day and a half.

Testis

Supersperm

One man's testes produce nearly 300 million sperm cells each day. This means that (in theory!) it would take only 23 men just one day to produce enough sperm to reproduce the entire world population.

The average person has around 100,000 hairs growing on his head, and loses and replaces 100 hairs a day.

On average we blink our eyes 9,365 times each day. A single blink lasts 0.15 seconds, so a day's total blinks for one person last 23 minutes. All the world's daily blinks would put us in the dark for 267,000 years.

Human tear production averages about a teaspoonful per day, although crying can spill that much out of the eyes all at once.

A day's beard growth for all the world's men would produce a beard 485 miles (780 km) long. If the daily shaving time of all the world's men were added up, it would produce a shave that lasted 30,000 years.

The human mouth has 3 pairs of salivary glands, which among them produce 2.1 pints (1 liter) of saliva a day.

The kidneys filter impurities from 951 gallons (3,600 liters) of blood every day. That's enough liquid to fill 45 bathtubs.

Food is liquidized in the stomach with the help of acids strong enough to dissolve zinc. It's no wonder that half a million cells lining the stomach die and must be replaced every minute.

It takes about 24 hours for food to travel the full length of the human digestive tract, which is 25 ft (7.5 m) long.

Red blood cells are created and destroyed at the rate of 2 million per second. That's 173 billion cells per person per day.

Nails grow at up to 0.004 in (0.1 mm) per day from a bed of active cells under the skin folds at the base and sides of a nail. Fingernails grow up to four times faster than toenails, and both grow faster in warm weather than in cold.

SMALL WORLD

The human body is host to many different kinds of microorganisms, including eyebrow mites and amoebas that swim on our teeth. Around 10 billion bacteria live on the skin and 15 trillion bacteria live in our digestive system.

Fleas can jump 14,400 times a day in search of food, and lay up to 1,000 eggs a day.

A tick can spend a whole day feeding on human blood, and then – after it drops off the skin – a whole year without feeding again.

Tapeworms can live in the small intestine. Every day, hundreds of eggs drop off the worm and are passed in the feces.

The head louse can live on the scalp. It lays up to 10 eggs, called nits, every day. Head lice feed on blood that they suck through the skin.

Mother's milk

A commercial dairy cow yields 38 pints (18 liters) of milk a day. It would take 25 nursing mothers to produce as much milk in one day as a single commercial dairy cow.

Grand flush

The body produces 3.6 pints (1.7 liters) of urine a day. The total daily world production of human urine would take a full 20 minutes to pass over Niagara Falls. If everyone in the world spent 5 minutes a day in the only bathroom in the world, that bathroom would be occupied for 57,000 years!

It wasn't I!

The human digestive system expels 4.2 pints (2 liters) of gas every day. The average fart is composed of 59% nitrogen, 21% hydrogen, 9% carbon dioxide, 7% methane, and 4% oxygen. That means the world releases enough hydrogen in its daily farts to fill 13 Hindenburg airships.

Around 1,000 brain cells are lost per head per day. But cell loss hardly slows down the nerve impulses of the brain, which travel at around 180 mph (290 kph).

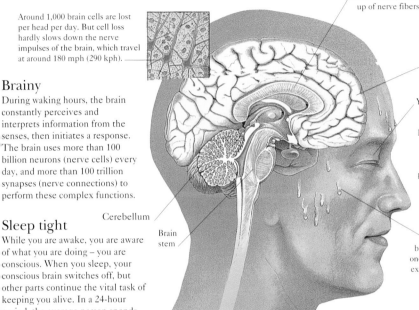

White matter, made up of nerve fibers

Frontal lobe of cerebrum

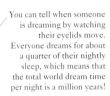

Brainy

During waking hours, the brain constantly perceives and interprets information from the senses, then initiates a response. The brain uses more than 100 billion neurons (nerve cells) every day, and more than 100 trillion synapses (nerve connections) to perform these complex functions.

Sleep tight

While you are awake, you are aware of what you are doing – you are conscious. When you sleep, your conscious brain switches off, but other parts continue the vital task of keeping you alive. In a 24-hour period, the average person spends seven hours asleep. The entire world population spends just over five million years asleep every night!

Cerebellum

Brain stem

You can tell when someone is dreaming by watching their eyelids move. Everyone dreams for about a quarter of their nightly sleep, which means that the total world dream time per night is a million years!

What a stink!

All the human excrement produced in one day would weigh about 1.1 million tons (1 million tonnes). It would fill the enormous Louisiana Superdome, New Orleans, to a depth of 62 ft (9 m).

Sweat glands are the body's cooling system. In one day the world's bodies exude enough sweat to fill 16 cargo ships.

Transatlantic nails

If all the world's finger- and toenails could be joined together to make one gigantic nail, in just one day it would grow almost from London to New York.

After not cutting his nails for 44 years, the average length of Indian Shindar Chillal's nails was 46 in (117 cm).

A male office worker needs to consume 2,400 Cal (10,080 kJ) every day.

A policeman on the beat needs to eat 2,800 Cal (11,760 kJ) every day.

A soldier needs his diet to supply at least 3,500 Cal (14,700 kJ) a day.

Eating for energy

The energy given by the food we eat is measured in calories (Cal) and kilojoules (kJ). Active people need more calories each day than people who sit to work, although the body burns energy even during sleep to keep the metabolism going.

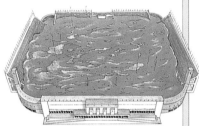

American operating rooms

American operating theaters are the busiest in the world. Around 197,000 operations take place in American hospitals every day. These include 1,679 hysterectomies, 381 hip replacements, 15,052 eye operations, 17,372 heart operations, 523 skin grafts, 285 brain operations, and 2,463 ear operations.

A DAY TO REMEMBER
Discovery of X ray

Photographic rays that pass through flesh but not through bone were discovered by William Röntgen on November 8, 1895, but not used medically until later.

First operation with anesthetic

On March 30, 1842, Dr. Crawford Long of Georgia, removed a cyst from the neck of James M. Venable using ether as an anesthetic.

First vaccination

On May 14, 1796, a British doctor, Dr. Edward Jenner, administered the first vaccination. Eight-year-old James Phipps was vaccinated with cowpox as protection against smallpox.

WORLD POPULATION

THE WORLD'S POPULATION IS EXPLODING FAST, with more people being born and living longer than ever before. By 1999, there were more than six billion people on Earth. The human boom is set to continue – especially in Africa, Asia, and Latin America – until, in 2080, it will peak at just over ten billion. The world's population first began to rocket about 10,000 years ago, when people began to grow their own food. The birth rate soared again in the West during the 1800s with the scientific advances of the Industrial Revolution. New methods of growing and transporting food meant that more people ate a better diet. There were also fewer deaths in childhood. Today, 12 times more people are added to the population of the world every day than would have been 100 years ago.

Growing fast
The expanding maps along the bottom of the page show how many people are added every day to the populations of the world's 12 fastest growing countries.

Expanding cities
In many parts of the world, people are moving from rural areas to cities to find work and a better standard of living. Some of the world's largest cities are bursting at the seams, with people living in slums or shanty towns on the outskirts. Mexico City has expanded from nine million people at its heart to 24 million people. Sao Paulo has grown from nine million at the center to 21.5 million, and Seoul from ten million to 19 million.

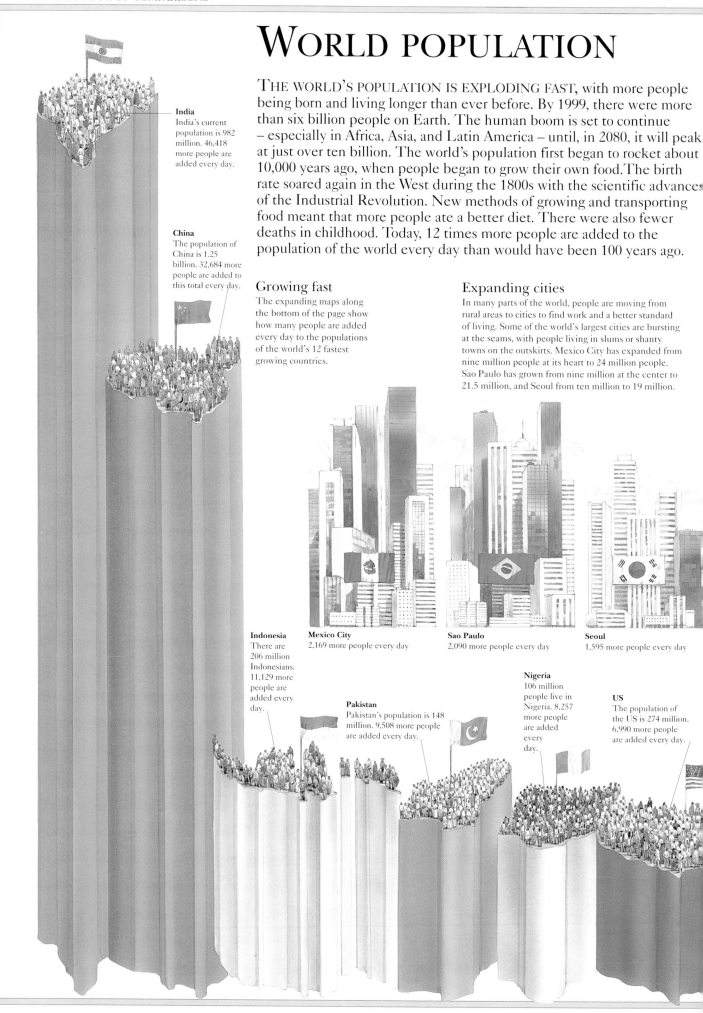

India
India's current population is 982 million. 46,418 more people are added every day.

China
The population of China is 1.25 billion. 32,684 more people are added to this total every day.

Indonesia
There are 206 million Indonesians. 11,129 more people are added every day.

Mexico City
2,169 more people every day

Sao Paulo
2,090 more people every day

Seoul
1,595 more people every day

Pakistan
Pakistan's population is 148 million. 9,508 more people are added every day.

Nigeria
106 million people live in Nigeria. 8,257 more people are added every day.

US
The population of the US is 274 million. 6,990 more people are added every day.

A DAY TO REMEMBER

Baby in a tube

The first test tube baby was Louise Brown. She was born in Oldham, in the UK, on July 25, 1978.

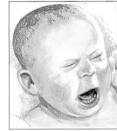

"We do!"

The largest ever wedding was conducted by Sun Myung Moon in Seoul, Korea, on August 25, 1995. He married 35,000 couples in the Olympic Stadium, and 325,000 other couples around the world by satellite link.

Cold as death

Dr. James Bedford was the first person to be frozen after death, on January 12, 1967, in accordance with the science of cryonics. His body will be defrosted when a cure is found for the illness that killed him.

ead end

ery day around the world,
arly 150,000 people take
eir last breath and die.
any die of old age, some
rish in accidents or are
urdered, while fatal
eases kill the rest.

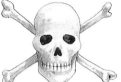

Heart disease
33,000 die every day.

Diarrhea
14,000 die every day.

Cancer
13,500 die every day.

A whale of a day

The total weight of all the 364,321 babies born in the world in one day is 760 tons (690 tonnes). This is the same weight as five blue whales.

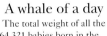

Pneumonia
13,500 die every day.

Tuberculosis
8,200 die every day.

Malaria
5,800 die
every day.

Measles
4,000 die
every day.

Whooping cough
1,400 die
every day.

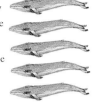

SMALL WORLD

China has more people than any other country on Earth, with a population of 1.2 billion. Overcrowding, and a shortage of resources including food, health care, and education, has caused the Chinese government to restrict family sizes in order to slow population growth rate. Chinese couples are encouraged to postpone marriage until their late 20s. In some areas, parents are allowed to have only one child.

Happy birthday!

Every day across the world, 16.5 million people celebrate their birthday. In many countries people mark the day with a feast or party. To mark a first birthday in Korea, the child is sat at a table with various objects on it – whichever he or she picks up is said to determine that child's future. Many Buddhists celebrate their birthdays by taking gifts of food to monks, and by releasing fish, turtles, and birds at the temple.

Births and deaths

In one day all over the world, 364,321 people are born and 147,137 people die. So every day there are 217,184 more people on Earth.

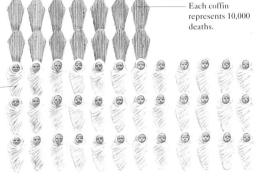

Each coffin represents 10,000 deaths.

Each baby in swaddling clothes represents 10,000 births.

Crowded planet

A hundred years from now, 378,000 people will be born every day, and 324,000 people will die. So every day, there will be 54,000 more people on Earth. In 1996 the world birth rate was 25 per 1,000, and the death rate, 9 per 1,000. In 2100, the World Bank predicts that the birth rate will be down to 13 per 1,000 and the death rate up to 11 per 1,000.

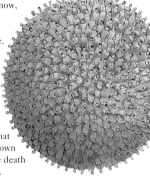

Brazil
166 million people live in Brazil. 6,757 more are added every day.

Bangladesh
Bangladesh has a population of 125 million. 6,186 more people are added every day.

Iran
66 million people live in Iran. 4,945 more people are added every day.

Mexico
Mexico has a population of 96 million. 4,789 more people are added every day.

Ethiopia
60 million people live in Ethiopia. 4,661 more people are added every day.

Vietnam
Vietnam's population is 78 million. 4,315 more people are added every day.

ONE DAY'S FOOD

IT WOULD TAKE 75 SUPERTANKERS to carry one day's food for the entire planet. Most people rely on wheat, rice, and corn for their basic food. Adults need about 2,500 calories of food energy a day. However, while Westerners consume up to 4,000 calories a day, some Africans survive on barely 1,800 calories each. And every day, 35,000 people die of starvation. Nutritious vegetables may hold the answer to the world's food needs. A field of soybeans yields 30 times more body-building protein than a field on which beef cattle are raised.

738,000 beef cattle are slaughtered every day.

The world slaughters almost 3 million pigs a day.

1.4 million sheep are slaughtered every day.

104 million chickens are slaughtered every day worldwide.

Meat
Every day, the world eats 665,800 tons (604,000 tonnes) of meat, the same weight as a herd of a million cows. But if everyone had a share of the world's meat, there would be barely enough for two mouthfuls a day each.

Food city
This is what the world's daily helpings of some of its most nutritious foodstuffs would look like, delivered into the heart of a modern city.

Potatoes
We dig up 744,059 tons (675,000 tonnes) of potatoes every day.

Beans and lentils
In one day, the world produces 172,000 tons (156,000 tonnes) of beans and lentils.

Grapes
The world's grape harvest for one day weighs 173,000 tons (157,000 tonnes) – that's 22 billion individual grapes.

Bananas
The world's daily banana harvest is 176,400 tons (160,000 tonnes).

Cabbages
The world produces 145,000 tons (132,000 tonnes) of cabbages in a day.

Watermelons
Every day 143,300 tons (130,000 tonnes) of watermelons are harvested.

Cocoa
The world produces 8,818 tons (8,000 tonnes) of cocoa beans every day. That's enough to make 700 million bars of chocolate.

Peas
Every day, the world harvests 20,900 tons (19,000 tonnes) of peas. That's enough to give 300 million people a serving of peas.

The fastest food in the world
Every day, Americans munch through 7 million pizzas, 4,400 tons (4,000 tonnes) of potato chips, 440 tons (400 tonnes) of pretzels, 300,000 cans of Spam, around 15 million burgers, 4 million gallons of ice cream, 250 million sodas, as well as 5 French fries each.

Fries
Soda
Burgers
Ice cream
Pretzels
Pizza

Tea
Worldwide, over 8,800 tons (8,000 tonnes) of tea leaves are produced every day. That's enough for 3 billion cups of tea.

Cucumbers
The world grows more than 80,000 tons (73,000 tonnes) of cucumbers every day. That's enough for everyone in India and China to have a cucumber sandwich.

Onions
The world's daily onion harvest weighs more than 121,000 tons (110,000 tonnes), as much as the largest ocean liner afloat.

Salt
The world harvests 551,155 tons (500,000 tonnes) of salt in a day.

Eggs
Eggs are a complete food because they provide all the proteins the body needs for tissue growth and repair. Today China is the world's biggest egg-producing nation. The world's hen population lays more than 2 billion eggs a day, which would make an omelette as big as the island of Cyprus.

Japan
The Japanese eat 27,557 tons (25,000 tonnes) of fish a day.

France
The French love the pungent flavor of garlic. France produces 138,000 tons (126 tonnes) of garlic every day.

China
The Chinese lead the world in rice production. They eat rice at every meal, going through 584,224 tons (530,000 tonnes) every day.

Greece
The Greeks eat more bread than anyone else in the world – 9 oz (300 g) per person per day.

Wheat
Wheat is one of the world's major food crops, with 1.8 million tons (1.6 million tonnes) harvested every day. The world eats enough wheat in one day to make a loaf as heavy as three Empire State Buildings.

Rice
More than 1.6 million tons (1.5 million tonnes) of rice is harvested every day, and about half of the world's population eats it as the main ingredient of meals. The world's daily helping of rice would make a heap as big as Egypt's Great Pyramid.

Tomatoes
All the tomatoes eaten in the world in one day weigh 271,000 tons (246,000 tonnes).

Corn
Every day 1.87 million tons (1.7 million tonnes) of corn is harvested, and the world eats enough corn to equal the weight of 300,000 African elephants.

Oranges
The orange is probably the world's most popular fruit – 198,000 tons (180,000 tonnes) are picked every day.

Pineapples
The world produces 37,000 tons (33,000 tonnes) of pineapples every day.

Sugar
The world produces 373,000 tons (339,000 tonnes) of sugar a day.

Apples
The world's daily apple harvest is 168,000 tons (153,000 tonnes).

Lemons and limes
In one day, the world produces 28,660 tons (26,000 tonnes) of lemons and limes.

Garlic
Every day 36,800 tons (33,000 tonnes) of garlic are produced worldwide.

Apricots
The world's daily apricot harvest weighs 7,716 tons (7,000 tonnes) and would fill 7 barges.

Avocados
The world avocado harvest weighs in at almost 6,613 tons (6,000 tonnes) a day.

Pumpkins
The world produces 44,000 tons (40,000 tonnes) of pumpkins in a day.

Mangoes
In one day the world produces more than 70,600 tons (64,000 tonnes) of mangoes.

Strawberries
The world's daily consumption of strawberries is 7,716 tons (7,000 tonnes).

Raspberries
The world produces 990 tons (900 tonnes) of raspberries every day – enough to fill a train pulling 23 cars.

Carrots
In one day the world produces 56,000 tons (51,000 tonnes) of carrots.

Coconuts
In a day the world produces 147,000 tons (131,000 tonnes) of coconuts.

Caviar
The world produces 3 tons (2.7 tonnes) of caviar in a day.

High-flying food
Nearly 3 million meals are served in the air every day.

Honey
In one day bees sip the nectar from 3 trillion flowers. They make 3,300 tons (3,000 tonnes) of honey, enough to cover a slice of toast as big as London.

OUT OF THIS WORLD
The first astronauts ate cold paste that they squeezed from a tube. Today's astronauts have a menu of more than 70 items. Some of these are in cans or foil bags. Others need to have water added. Many are heated before eating. Astronauts eat from trays strapped to their laps.

PRODUCTION

THE WORLD IS A MIGHTY PRODUCTION machine, every day its factories and offices churn out billions of dollars worth of "stuff." It's strange to think that machines were invented less than 300 years ago, and before that time, everything was made at home, by hand. The first machines were powered by renewable energy – the sweat of human effort, and water turning a wheel. But the age of steam was fired by coal, so the first really efficient machines began to gobble up Earth's natural resources. Today the world uses the equivalent of 8 lb (4 kg) of oil per person a day – though Americans consume 5¹⁄₂ times that amount!

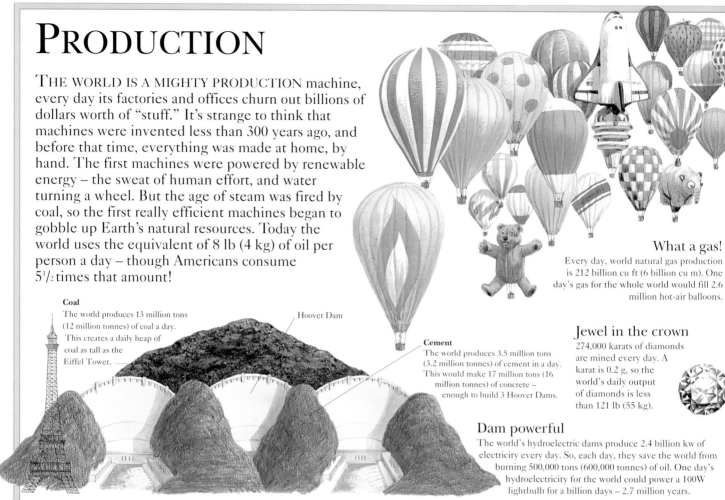

What a gas!
Every day, world natural gas production is 212 billion cu ft (6 billion cu m). One day's gas for the whole world would fill 2.6 million hot-air balloons.

Coal
The world produces 13 million tons (12 million tonnes) of coal a day. This creates a daily heap of coal as tall as the Eiffel Tower.

Hoover Dam

Cement
The world produces 3.5 million tons (3.2 million tonnes) of cement in a day. This would make 17 million tons (16 million tonnes) of concrete – enough to build 3 Hoover Dams.

Jewel in the crown
274,000 karats of diamonds are mined every day. A karat is 0.2 g, so the world's daily output of diamonds is less than 121 lb (55 kg).

Dam powerful
The world's hydroelectric dams produce 2.4 billion kw of electricity every day. So, each day, they save the world from burning 500,000 tons (600,000 tonnes) of oil. One day's hydroelectricity for the world could power a 100W lightbulb for a billion days – 2.7 million years.

Black gold
The world produces almost 9.92 million tons (9 million tonnes) of oil a day, which is enough to fill the holds of 90 cargo ships. Every day in the world's refineries, 2.5 million tons (2.3 million tonnes) of oil is turned into gas, and 1.5 million tons (1.4 million tonnes) is used to manufacture plastics.

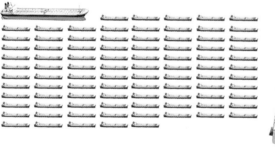

Cars, cars, cars
Every day, a staggering 141,132 vehicles roll off the world's production lines. The US is the world's biggest car manufacturer, but the people of Luxembourg own more cars per head than any other nation in the world. In Luxembourg there are 57 cars on the road for every 100 people.

Crude wealth
A typical oil rig can pump up 189,000 barrels of precious crude oil from the Earth every day.

Neon city
A nuclear power station could produce enough electricity in a day to supply the city of Las Vegas for 8 years.

US
The US produces 32,326 vehicles a day.

Japan
Japan manufactures 28,345 vehicles every day.

France
The French manufacture 9,837 vehicles daily.

Germany
13,268 vehicles roll off Germany's production lines each day.

South Korea
In South Korea, 7,706 vehicles are produced every day.

Canada
Every day Canada's factories produce over 6,567 vehicles.

Spain
Spain manufactures 6,609 vehicles a day.

UK
5,272 vehicles roll out of the assembly plant every day in the UK.

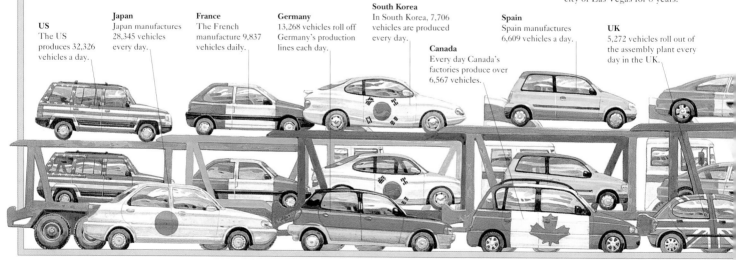

Awesome ores

Metals are extracted from ores – naturally occurring minerals that are mined from the Earth.

The world produces 55,000 tons (50,000 tonnes) of copper every day. That would make enough copper piping to encircle the globe 3 times.

80,300 tons (72,847 tonnes) of aluminum are produced in a day, enough to make almost 5 billion soda cans.

The world's mines yield 99 tons (90 tonnes) of uranium every day. Uranium is used to power nuclear reactors.

Daily world production of platinum is 176 lb (80 kg). It is used in electrical instruments and jewelry.

The world output of mercury is 12 tons (11 tonnes) a day, enough to fill nearly 7 million thermometers.

Gold rush

7.44 tons (6.75 tonnes) of gold is mined in one day – more than a quarter of it comes from South Africa. Gold is so dense that the world's daily gold extraction could fit inside a refrigerator. Every day, 330 lb (150 kg) of gold (much of it recycled) is used to fill teeth – that's the weight of more than 2 adults.

A new car every day

The number of cars in the world is increasing at a little more than half the rate of world population growth. Every day, at least one new car is produced for every other additional person on the planet.

Italy
4,234 vehicles are manufactured in Italy every day.

Brazil
Brazil produces 4,966 vehicles daily.

MONEY WORLD

The world's banks send money to each other 24 hours a day. Instead of cash, they transmit computer messages giving the amount. In one day, banks exchange over 1.5 million electronic messages. In this way, about $2 trillion moves around the globe every day. As well as money itself, the global financial markets trade in stocks and bonds, which may be shares in business companies. The total value of the world's tradable stocks and bonds is $8.5 trillion.

Great heaps of stuff

If all the tons of different stuff produced in the world in a single day could be piled up into heaps, the landscape would be dominated by mountains of useful goods. The daily powdered laundry detergent pile would be big enough to ski down, and one day's timber pile would reach up into outer space.

Steel
Around 3.3 million tons (2 million tonnes) of steel is produced every day. If all this steel was turned into cars, it would make 2.5 million vehicles in one day.

Computers
IBM manufactures 20,000 computers a day.

Soap powder
59,000 tons (54,000 tonnes) of soap and laundry detergent are produced in a day. That would be enough to wash 2 loads of laundry for each US citizen.

Washing machines
The world churns out 101,000 washing machines a day.

Tires
2.3 million tires are manufactured every day, almost a quarter of them in the US.

Refrigerators
Worldwide, 137,000 refrigerators are made every day.

String
If you made the world's daily harvest of around 11,000 tons (10,000 tonnes) of jute, sisal, and hemp into string, it would be 4 million miles (6.5 million km) long. It would stretch 17 times from the Earth to the Moon.

Timber
Worldwide, enough timber is cut every day to produce 150 million planks of wood. If all the logs cut in a day were used to build a tower, it would reach up into outer space.

"This pile of timber was built in one day, and it reaches up into space – or so they tell me!"

"I'll sleep like a log after building this tower!"

"This is the cleanest ski slope I've ever seen!"

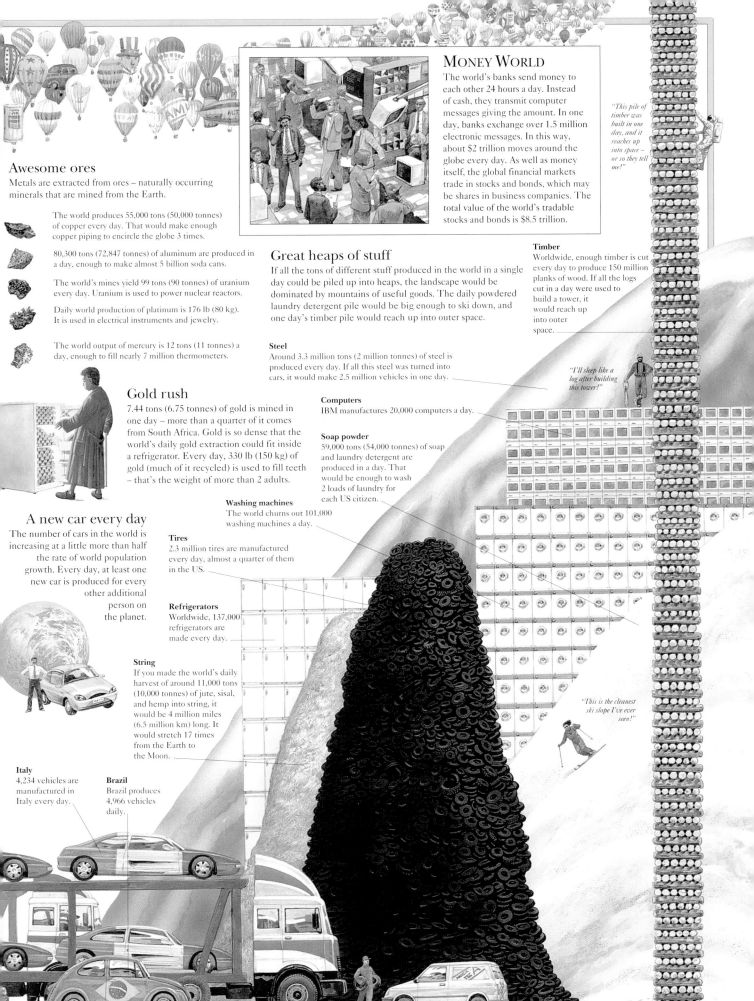

WASTE AND RECYCLING

RECYCLING GARBAGE MEANS that we take fewer raw materials from the Earth. Recycling paper the world over eliminates the need to cut down five million trees every day. Recycling also helps to save energy. With the amount of energy needed to make one aluminum can from raw materials, 20 can be made from recycled aluminum. Most household waste can be recycled. Kitchen scraps can be composted, and glass taken to a bottle bank to be crushed and melted down to make new glass. Plastics can be shredded, melted, and reformed.

Clear glass

Ash and dust

Paper

Newspaper

Kitchen waste

Magazines, diapers, plastic film, clothing

Miscellaneous waste

Wasteful house

In one day, the average British household generates 4 lb (1.74 kg) of garbage pail waste. In a year, this grows to the equivalent of the weight of 11 adults.

Diaper mountain

Babies in the US go through 8,267 tons (7,500 tonnes) of disposable diapers every day. A day's worth of soiled diapers would fill 100,000 garbage pails. Piled up, they would make a mountain as big as a 10-story building.

Deforestation

Every day, enough tropical rain forest is cut down to cover an island as big as Barbados. During the 1980s, an area of forest was cut down that would have completely covered Germany.

One 40-ft (12-m) tree will make a stack of newspapers 4 ft (1.2 m) high.

The number of trees felled in one day around the world would cover the island of Barbados.

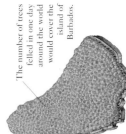

The US uses enough water in one day for each of its citizens to take 64 baths.

World garbage

If everyone in the world produced garbage at the rate of the average American, the world garbage dump would grow by 13.2 million tons (12 million tonnes) a day – equivalent to a herd of 2.4 million elephants. Fortunately, the world's garbage heap grows by a mere 2.2 million tons (two million tonnes) every day.

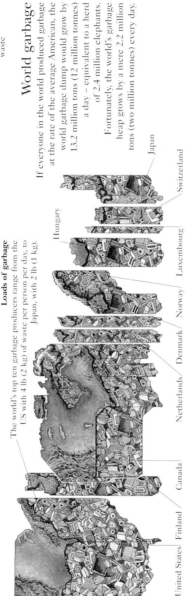

Japan

Switzerland

Hungary

Luxembourg

Norway

Denmark

Netherlands

Canada

United States   Finland

Loads of garbage

The world's top ten garbage producers range from the US with 4 lb (2 kg) of waste per person per day, to Japan, with 2 lb (1 kg).

Composted
20,392 tons
(18,500 tonnes)

Composted
1,102 tons
(1,000 tonnes)

Incinerated
89,287 tons
(81,000 tonnes)

Incinerated
48,501 tons
(44,000 tonnes)

Recycled
114,640 tons
(104,000 tonnes)

Recycled
48,501 tons
(44,000 tonnes)

Landfill
348,881 tons
(316,500 tonnes)

Landfill
22,000 tons
(20,000 tonnes)

United States

Japan

US and Japan

Every day in the US, 573,201 tons (520,000 tonnes) of garbage is produced. A fifth of that garbage – 114,640 tons (104,000 tonnes) – is recycled. In Japan, 120,151 tons (109,000 tonnes) of garbage is produced in one day. Japan recycles almost half its garbage – 48,501 tons (44,000 tonnes) every day. Yet both countries are still very wasteful. Japan dumps 82,000 disposable plastic cameras every day. In the US, 685,000 cu ft (19,000 cu m) of loose plastic "peanuts" are used in packaging every day – that's enough to fill 43 American homes or the passenger

Piles of waste

The large illustration shows waste and recycling figures for paper, cars, newspaper, kitchen appliances, tires, cans, and clothes. The US and Japan lag behind Germany, which has strict laws about recycling. It recycles about 22,000 tons (20,000 tonnes) of packaging materials in one day.

Paper in the US

In one day, the US throws away 222,666 tons (202,000 tonnes) of paper, of which 77,161 tons (70,000 tonnes) is recycled.

Paper in Japan

Japan uses 77,161 tons (70,000 tonnes) of paper in one day, and recycles more than half of it.

Cars

In the US, 35,280 tons (32,000 tonnes) of cars are put on the scrap heap every day. 26455 tons (24,000 tonnes) of materials from them are recycled.

Newspapers

30,000 tons (28,000 tonnes) of newsprint is dumped every day in the USA, of which 14,330 tons (13,000 tonnes) is recycled. Each Sunday edition of the *New York Times* produces 3,968 tons (3,600 tonnes) of waste.

The world average consumption of water is one third that of the US.

Toxic waste

Vegetation in many areas of the US has been damaged by acid rain. This is because the US releases almost 3,306 tons (3,000 tonnes) of toxic chemicals into the atmosphere in one day. That's a whole load of poisonous chemicals, weighing as much as 15 Statues of Liberty every single day.

"Sacre bleu! That's not on my navigation chart!"

Sea dumping

Every day, 20,000 tons (18,000 tonnes) of litter is chucked into the world's seas – the same weight as two Eiffel Towers or 136 blue whales. That garbage includes 450,000 nonbiodegradable plastic containers.

Enough for a bath

In the Western world, everyone uses about 30 gallons (135 liters) of water every day just to flush the toilet. That's enough for one and a half baths.

"I'm flushing away all my worries!"

Water everywhere

The world average consumption of water is 22 bathfuls per person per day. For each person, two bathfuls are used in the home, five by industry, and 15 by agriculture. The US uses enough water every day for each of its citizens to take 64 baths. Eight bathfuls of water per person are used in the home, 27 by agriculture, and 29 by industry. Yet 1.2 billion people in the developing world lack safe drinking water.

Oil spillage

The amount of oil spilled in the sea and on land in one day would fill up five Olympic-sized swimming pools.

Steel cans

13 million steel cans are recycled every day in the US. That's 9,000 steel cans every minute of the day, or 150 a second!

Cans have wings

All the aluminum cans thrown out in one day in the US would build 16 DC-10 airliners.

Released into the atmosphere 69 %

Dumped into surface water 3 %

Deposited on land 13 %

Buried underground 15 %

Dumping ground
This cross section shows where toxic waste is dumped.

Kitchen appliances
In one day, the US dumps 9,259 tons (8,400 tonnes) of large kitchen appliances. 5,180 tons (4,700 tonnes) of materials from them are recycled.

Rubber tires
8,157 tons (7,400 tonnes) of tires are dumped every day in the US. More than 1,102 tons (1,000 tonnes) of them are recycled.

Aluminum cans
4,684 tons (4,250 tonnes) of aluminum are thrown out in the US every day, and 3,064 tons (2,780 tonnes) are recycled.

Clothing
2,866 tons (2,600 tonnes) of clothing are scrapped every day in the US. Hardly any is recycled.

Aluminum cans in Japan
Japan uses 881 tons (800 tonnes) of aluminum cans every day, and recycles 577 tons (523 tonnes).

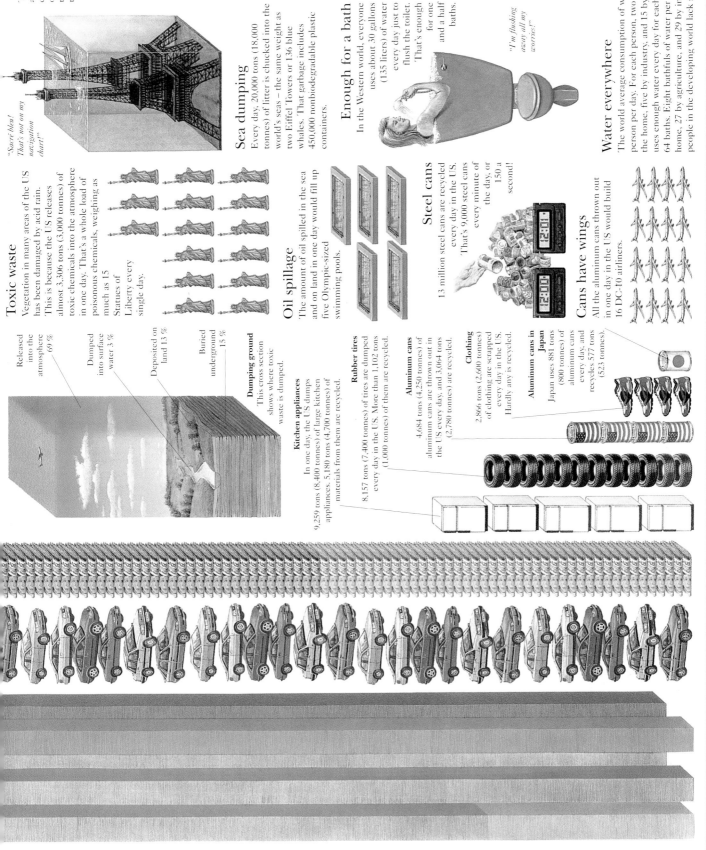

COMMUNICATIONS

WORDS WERE FIRST SPOKEN by human mouths into human ears around 40,000 years ago. Today words can reach destinations on the other side of the globe almost as soon as they are uttered. Radio signals are bounced back to receiving stations by Earth's atmosphere, and satellites in space allow people to talk to each other, face to face, day and night, all across the planet. Our voices have escaped into space in the form of radio waves, and our first words have traveled 100 light years from the Earth. We have also beamed out messages, hoping to get in touch with alien beings – but as yet, no signal has been received from other worlds.

How satellite communications work
High-frequency signals for telephone, computer, and television pass straight through Earth's atmosphere. They need satellites in space to bounce them back to Earth. The higher the satellite, the greater the area of Earth it can cover.

UOSAT 12
Each day, University of Surrey Satellite 12 travels around the Earth 16 times. It is testing a propulsion system that uses steam instead of poisonous gas.

OPTUS B
Optus B travels 540,000 miles (864,000 km) each day, providing Australia and the Pacific with telephone and broadcasting links.

European weather satellite

Defense Support Program
DSP is a US missile-warning satellite. Its infrared sensors can detect hot exhaust from a nuclear missile. It photographs some part of the Earth's surface six times every minute, which comes to 8,640 photographs a day.

SOHO
Every day, SOHO (Solar and Heliospheric Observatory) measures millions of sunquakes or vibrations on the surface of the Sun.

Iridium
This is one of a series of 66 low-Earth orbit communications satellites launched in 1997. Each day, Iridium can transfer thousands of calls from mobile phones.

Infrared Space Observatory
Each day, the tank of supercold helium in ISO cools instruments to –455.8°F(–271°C), and allows them to measure tiny amounts of heat arriving from planets, gas clouds, and galaxies.

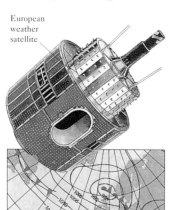

Meteosat
This Meteosat craft hovers over the Atlantic Ocean, from where it can "see" Europe's weather coming. Every day, it observes cloud movement, so weather forecasters can predict the weather for several days ahead.

Molniya
Molniya provides communications coverage (television and telephone calls) for the most northerly regions of Russia for about 8 hours every day.

Space Shuttle
In one day, the space shuttle can carry a crew of seven astronauts around the world 16 times, while they service and repair other craft, carry out scientific experiments, or take hundreds of photos of Earth.

"Sorry, wrong galaxy!"

Is anyone out there?
Radio telescopes on Earth are listening day and night for messages from space, but after almost 40 years, not one has been picked up! In 1974 we sent a message to a distant star cluster from Arecibo Observatory, Puerto Rico, the world's biggest radio telescope. It will be the 270th century before it gets there, and the 520th century before we could receive a reply!

Pioneer 10
The space probe Pioneer 10 was the first spacecraft to cross the asteroid belt and fly past Jupiter. It is now 9.7 billion miles (15.6 billion km) from Earth. Every day it travels 334,000 miles (536,000 km) into space.

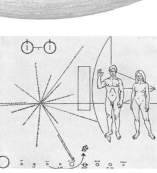

Message to other worlds
On its side, Pioneer 10 carries a plaque showing human figures and a diagram of the Earth's position in the universe. It is hoped that one day aliens will find the craft and communicate with Earth.

Letters from America

US
The US handles 520 million pieces of mail in one day.

The world sends 1.2 billion letters through the mail every day. If all these letters could be stacked together, they would make a bridge that would span the Atlantic Ocean.

UK
The UK handles around 52 million pieces of mail a day – that's one letter every day for each of the inhabitants of the British Isles.

SMALL WORLD

The Pentagon, Arlington, Virginia, is the headquarters of the American Department of Defense. It has one of the world's largest private telephone systems, with 34,500 individual lines, handling a million calls a day. It also has the world's largest pneumatic tube system, with 15 miles (24 km) of tube, through which letters are transported by means of air pressure.

HALCA
This Japanese radio astronomy satellite travels around Earth 4 times every day.

With love from me to you

Christmas Day is celebrated in the US with 2.7 billion festive cards. And one million romantic Americans lick stamps each year to make the mail for Valentine's Day on February 14.

INTELSAT 8
Each day, Intelsats are able to relay up to 112,500 two-way telephone conversations at the same time, as well as 3 television channels.

Stampede

Americans stick about 13.7 million stamps every day. Pasted edge to edge, they would cover 2 American football fields.

"I know a secret, but my lips are sealed!"

"I'm out of the country right now."

'Allo? 'Allo?

Every day, 730 million telephone lines and more than 200 million mobile phones are in use across the world. Most of the talking goes on in North America. The average American makes 5 calls a day. If the total daily calls between the US and Canada were added up into a single conversation, they would make a telephone call that lasted 23 years!

"Your Shuttle needs a tune-up, buddy."

NAVSTAR
NAVSTAR is a series of 24 navigation satellites. Each satellite travels around the Earth twice a day, sending signals that help boats and planes locate their positions.

ACTS
The Advanced Communications Technology Satellite takes exactly 24 hours to orbit the Earth as it spins on its axis.

"Salut!"

"Hello!"

"Bore da!"

"Jambo!"

"Iska warran!"

"Hej!"

"Ciao!"

Hubble Space Telescope
Each day, HST takes pictures of planets, stars, dust clouds, black holes, and quasars. With new cameras fitted in 1997, HST can see far back into the past, detecting the first galaxies soon after they were born.

Computer-speak

Computers were first used for communications in 1969 by scientists and academics. Now, there are more than 160 million users talking to each other every day on the Internet.

"Dumela!"

Let's chat

Every day, people around the world communicate with each other in thousands of different languages, each with its own culture and traditions.

"Hoi!"

"Alo!"

"Kumusta!"

"Bloomin' bootiful!"

Don't shoot the messenger

Every business day, Federal Express delivers more than 2 million items to over 200 countries around the world.

Flower power

Every day, the British communicate happiness, sympathy, or regret by sending 11,000 bunches of flowers.

A DAY TO REMEMBER

Dots and dashes

On January 8, 1838, the first Morse Code message was sent by a student of Samuel Morse. It read: "A patient waiter is no loser."

Altitude problem

The ballpoint pen was patented on June 10, 1943, by László Josef Biró. It was used by navigators, because fountain pens leak at altitude, and pencils do not mark weatherproof maps.

Royal cable

On August 16, 1858, Queen Victoria sent a formal greeting to American President James Buchanan. She was the first head of state to use the world's first transatlantic cable.

TRAVEL

IF ALL THE FOOTSTEPS TAKEN IN THE WORLD in one day could be put together to make one long journey, the human race could walk 88 times to the Sun and back every 24 hours. On wheels, wings, water, and on foot, this restless world is constantly on the move. Traveling is more comfortable for some than for others. In the West, there is a car for every two people. In Ethiopia, there is only one car for every 1,468 people.

World flights
Every day there are 45,000 scheduled flights carrying more than 3.5 million passengers. This is equivalent to the total population of Puerto Rico taking to the skies.

On the go all day
How far could the different forms of transportation in this fleet travel in a day if each one maintained its maximum cruising speed over a 24-hour period? In reality, of course, fuel tanks would run dry, engines would overheat, and stamina would flag long before the day was out.

Passenger helicopter
Cruises at 150 mph (241 kph). In 24 hours, it could travel 3,600 miles (5,784 km).

Concorde
Cruises at 1,450 mph (2,222 kph). In 24 hours, it could cover 34,800 miles (53,328 km).

Boeing 747-400
Cruises at 560 mph (901 kph). In 24 hours, it could travel 13,440 miles (21,624 km).

SeaCat ferry
Cruises at 40 mph (64 kph). In 24 hours, it could cover 960 miles (1,536 km).

Gas balloon
Travels at 10 mph (16 kph). In 24 hours, it could cover 240 miles (384 km).

Hovercraft
Travels at 75 mph (120 kph). In 24 hours, it could cover 1,800 miles (2,880 km).

Japanese Series E2 train
Cruises at 171 mph (275 kph). In 24 hours, it could cover 4,104 miles (6,600 km).

Motorcycle
Can cruise at 80 mph (129 kmh). In 24 hours it could cover 1,920 miles (3,096 km).

Heathrow Airport
London's Heathrow Airport has more international passengers than any other airport in the world. On an average day, it handles 105,000 passengers, 2,204 tons of freight – which might include racing cars and racehorses, as well as exotic fruit and vegetables – and 220 tons (200 tonnes) of mail. Every day, 1,200 aircraft land and take off. The airport's busiest day so far was June 30, 1995, when 194,500 passengers passed through it.

European bus and personnel carrier
Both these vehicles can cruise along the highway at 70 mph (113 kph). In 24 hours they would cover 1,680 miles (2,712 km).

Personnel carrier

93 different airlines operate at Heathrow.

Every day, 35,000 of Heathrow's passengers travel on to a further destination.

Each aircraft holds an average of 130 passengers.

Every day, Heathrow has 36 flights to Paris and 22 flights to New York.

156,000 items of baggage pass through Heathrow Airport every day.

Every day, 40–50 Very Important Persons get special treatment as they pass through the airport.

Heathrow's cafés and bars sell 26,000 cups of tea and coffee, 6,500 pints of beer, and 6,500 sandwiches every day.

BRITISH AIRWAYS

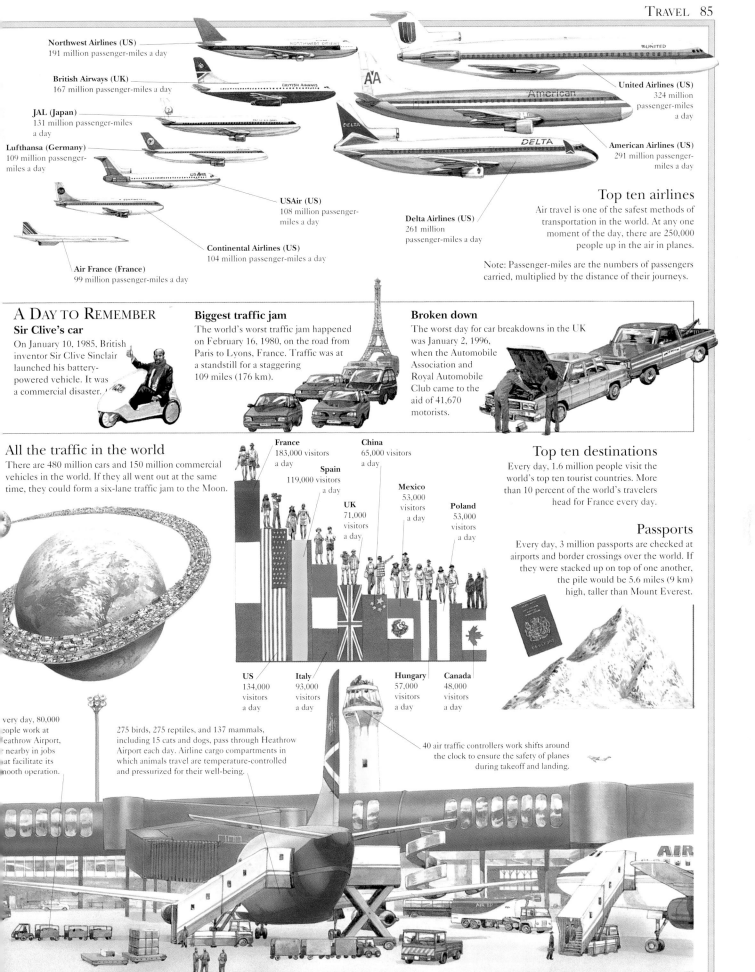

Northwest Airlines (US)
191 million passenger-miles a day

British Airways (UK)
167 million passenger-miles a day

JAL (Japan)
131 million passenger-miles a day

Lufthansa (Germany)
109 million passenger-miles a day

USAir (US)
108 million passenger-miles a day

Continental Airlines (US)
104 million passenger-miles a day

Air France (France)
99 million passenger-miles a day

United Airlines (US)
324 million passenger-miles a day

American Airlines (US)
291 million passenger-miles a day

Delta Airlines (US)
261 million passenger-miles a day

Top ten airlines
Air travel is one of the safest methods of transportation in the world. At any one moment of the day, there are 250,000 people up in the air in planes.

Note: Passenger-miles are the numbers of passengers carried, multiplied by the distance of their journeys.

A DAY TO REMEMBER
Sir Clive's car
On January 10, 1985, British inventor Sir Clive Sinclair launched his battery-powered vehicle. It was a commercial disaster.

Biggest traffic jam
The world's worst traffic jam happened on February 16, 1980, on the road from Paris to Lyons, France. Traffic was at a standstill for a staggering 109 miles (176 km).

Broken down
The worst day for car breakdowns in the UK was January 2, 1996, when the Automobile Association and Royal Automobile Club came to the aid of 41,670 motorists.

All the traffic in the world
There are 480 million cars and 150 million commercial vehicles in the world. If they all went out at the same time, they could form a six-lane traffic jam to the Moon.

France
183,000 visitors a day

Spain
119,000 visitors a day

UK
71,000 visitors a day

China
65,000 visitors a day

Mexico
53,000 visitors a day

Poland
53,000 visitors a day

US
134,000 visitors a day

Italy
93,000 visitors a day

Hungary
57,000 visitors a day

Canada
48,000 visitors a day

Top ten destinations
Every day, 1.6 million people visit the world's top ten tourist countries. More than 10 percent of the world's travelers head for France every day.

Passports
Every day, 3 million passports are checked at airports and border crossings over the world. If they were stacked up on top of one another, the pile would be 5.6 miles (9 km) high, taller than Mount Everest.

very day, 80,000 eople work at eathrow Airport, nearby in jobs at facilitate its nooth operation.

275 birds, 275 reptiles, and 137 mammals, including 15 cats and dogs, pass through Heathrow Airport each day. Airline cargo compartments in which animals travel are temperature-controlled and pressurized for their well-being.

40 air traffic controllers work shifts around the clock to ensure the safety of planes during takeoff and landing.

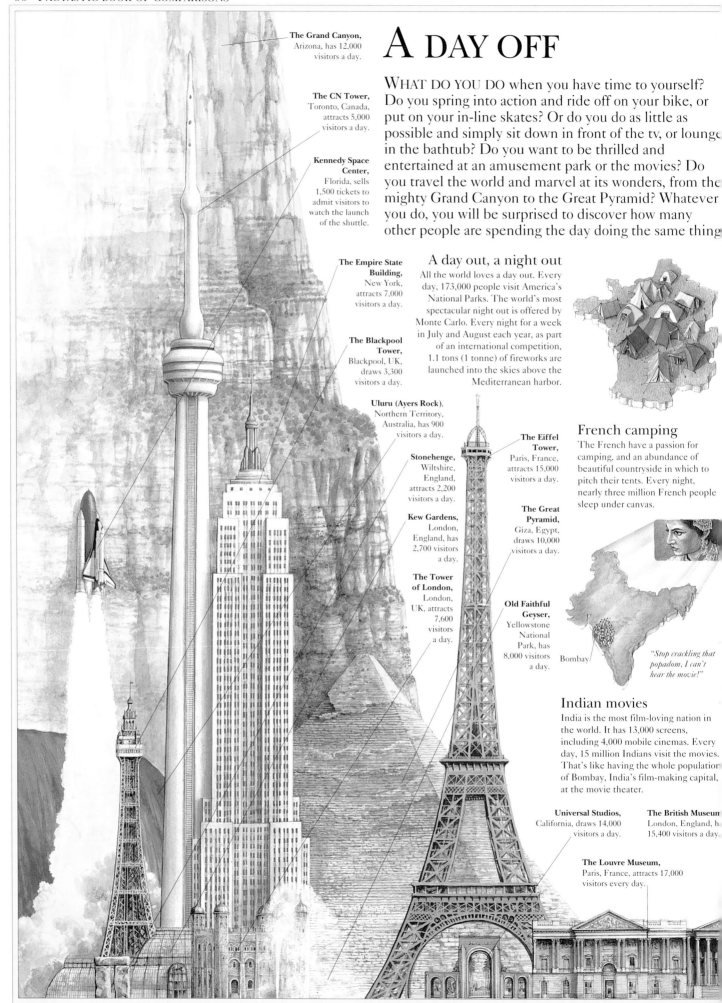

A DAY OFF

WHAT DO YOU DO when you have time to yourself? Do you spring into action and ride off on your bike, or put on your in-line skates? Or do you do as little as possible and simply sit down in front of the tv, or lounge in the bathtub? Do you want to be thrilled and entertained at an amusement park or the movies? Do you travel the world and marvel at its wonders, from the mighty Grand Canyon to the Great Pyramid? Whatever you do, you will be surprised to discover how many other people are spending the day doing the same thing

A day out, a night out

All the world loves a day out. Every day, 173,000 people visit America's National Parks. The world's most spectacular night out is offered by Monte Carlo. Every night for a week in July and August each year, as part of an international competition, 1.1 tons (1 tonne) of fireworks are launched into the skies above the Mediterranean harbor.

French camping

The French have a passion for camping, and an abundance of beautiful countryside in which to pitch their tents. Every night, nearly three million French people sleep under canvas.

"Stop crackling that popadom, I can't hear the movie!"

Bombay

Indian movies

India is the most film-loving nation in the world. It has 13,000 screens, including 4,000 mobile cinemas. Every day, 15 million Indians visit the movies. That's like having the whole population of Bombay, India's film-making capital, at the movie theater.

The Grand Canyon, Arizona, has 12,000 visitors a day.

The CN Tower, Toronto, Canada, attracts 5,000 visitors a day.

Kennedy Space Center, Florida, sells 1,500 tickets to admit visitors to watch the launch of the shuttle.

The Empire State Building, New York, attracts 7,000 visitors a day.

The Blackpool Tower, Blackpool, UK, draws 3,300 visitors a day.

Uluru (Ayers Rock), Northern Territory, Australia, has 900 visitors a day.

Stonehenge, Wiltshire, England, attracts 2,200 visitors a day.

Kew Gardens, London, England, has 2,700 visitors a day.

The Tower of London, London, UK, attracts 7,600 visitors a day.

The Eiffel Tower, Paris, France, attracts 15,000 visitors a day.

The Great Pyramid, Giza, Egypt, draws 10,000 visitors a day.

Old Faithful Geyser, Yellowstone National Park, has 8,000 visitors a day.

Universal Studios, California, draws 14,000 visitors a day.

The British Museum, London, England, has 15,400 visitors a day.

The Louvre Museum, Paris, France, attracts 17,000 visitors every day.

Golf crazy

The world has 28 million golfers. If they all went out on the same day, it would be like having the population of Tanzania on the golf course. There are more golfers per head in Japan than anywhere else in the world. Every day, 450,000 of them play golf on a course, and because space is limited in Japan, 850,000 Japanese thwack balls every day on indoor driving ranges.

"I'm gonna hit that ball all the way to Timbuktu."

New Zealand and Ireland
132,000 golfers

Scotland
220,000 golfers

Australia
374,000 golfers

England
495,000 golfers

Japan
8 million golfers

US
18 million golfers

Golf balls

More than 820,000 golf balls are sold worldwide every day. More than half of them are bought by Japanese golfers!

Exercise nation

Americans are the most health-conscious people in the world. Millions of them regularly huff and puff through energetic sports and exercise routines. For 70 million Americans, the favorite way of keeping trim and fit is to walk or jog. A staggering 20 million Americans participate in in-line skating.

58 million Americans get in the swim.

50 million Americans get on their bikes.

"What a sweat!"

46 million Americans lift weights or use other exercise equipment, in gyms or at home.

"Gotta get that ball in that net!"

40 million Americans go bowling.

29.4 million Americans play basketball.

0   10 million   20 million   30 million   40 million   50 million   60 million

Japan
9 hours television a day

US
7 hours television a day

UK
3 hours 35 minutes television a day

Canada
3 hours 24 minutes television a day

Germany
2 hours 13 minutes television a day

France
2 hours 9 minutes television a day

Italy
2 hours 4 minutes television a day

Denmark
1 hour 54 minutes television a day

Glued to the tube

In many homes in the Western world, the glowing picture box at the heart of the house is hardly ever turned off. First there were tv dinners, then came breakfast time tv. Now people who live tv lives can also shop and bank through the tube.

A DAY TO REMEMBER
Royal wedding

The biggest television audience ever – 750 million people around the world – tuned in to watch the wedding of the Prince and Princess of Wales on July 29, 1981. Two hundred and fifty million people listened on the radio and 500,000 lined the streets of London to watch the event live.

Carry on karaoke

Every day in Japan, 800,000 people sing karaoke in public. In the United States, more than three million recordings – including two million CDs – are sold in just one day. The UK sells 800,000 recordings a day.

US
3 million recordings a day

UK
800,000 recordings a day

Paris Air Show,
326,000 visitors in one day. The air show takes place every two years in June.

Carnival,
Rio de Janeiro, Brazil. 50,000 people parade through the streets in costume every day during the carnival.

Disneyland,
Tokyo, Japan. 45,700 people visit the world's most popular Disneyland every day.

Niagara Falls,
Canada/US. Every day, 30,000 people visit the spectacular waterfalls.

"Help! I feel sick!"

INDEX

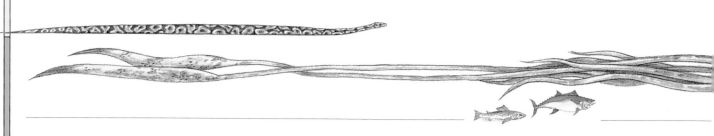

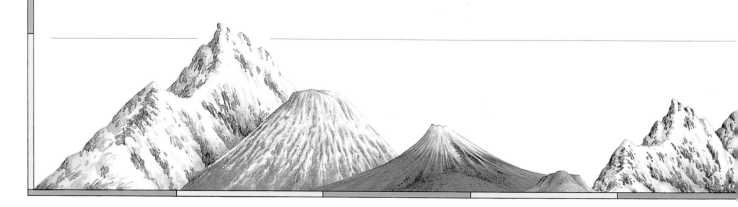

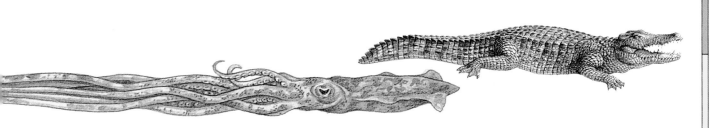

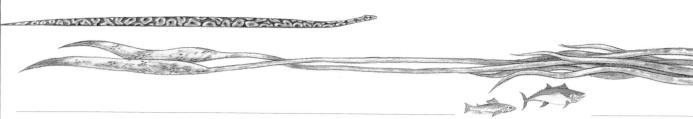

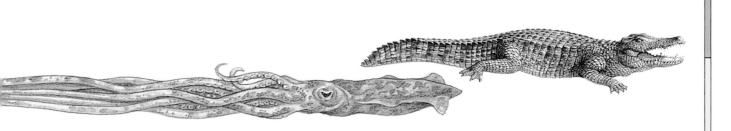

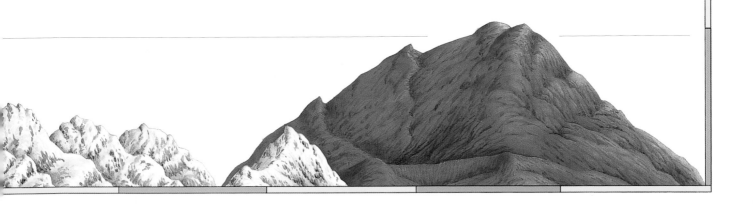

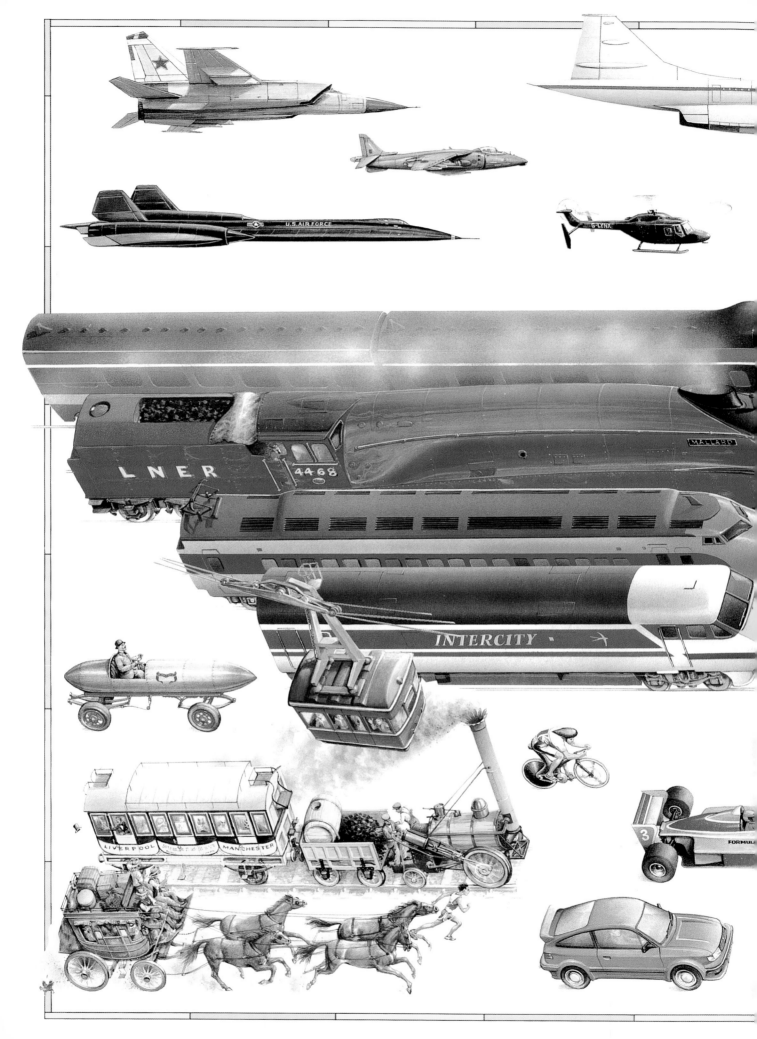

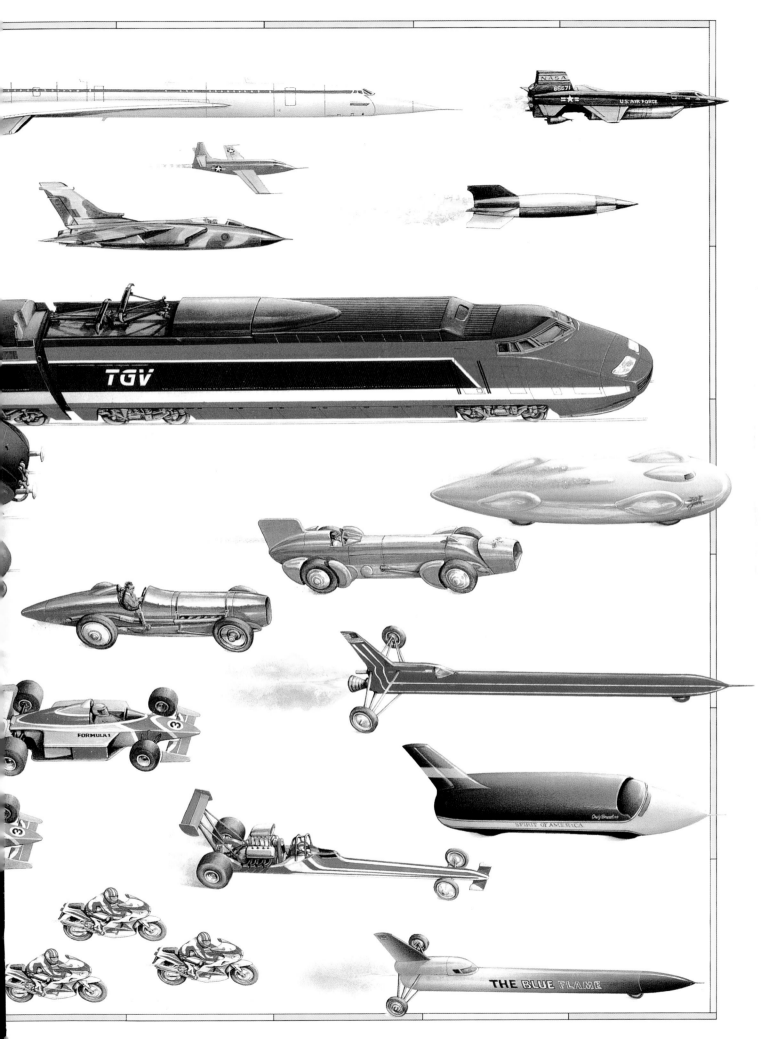

TGV

FORMULA 1

SPIRIT OF AMERICA

THE BLUE FLAME

ACKNOWLEDGMENTS

**Dorling Kindersley would like to thank
the following for helping with this book –**

Design: Jo Earl, Jim Miles, Sheilagh Noble, Simon Faires

Editorial: Terry Martin, Richard Platt, Phil Wilkinson, Francesca
Baines, Robert Graham, Angela Koo, Nichola Roberts

Index: Chris Bernstein

Illustrations: Russell Barnett, Michael Courtney, Angelika
Elsbach, Richard Bonson, Stephen Conlin, Peter Dennis (Linda
Rogers Associates), Chris Forsey, Malcolm Mcgregor, and Peter
Visscher

Research: Professor John Allen; Amateur Yacht Research
Society; Cameron Balloons; Carluccio's; Chicago Bridge & Iron
Company; Dr Peter Cotgreave, London Zoo; Edificio Petróleos
de Venezuela; Robert Graham; Hapag Lloyd; Kitty Hauser;
Esther Labi; Lindstrand Balloons; Lloyd's List; Keith Lye;
Natural History Museum; P & O; Steve Parker;
Royal Botanic Gardens, Kew;
Silja Shipping; World Sailing Records

Additional acknowledgments: The Automobile Association;
Biosphere II; Peter Bond; Gary Booth; Heathrow Airport; Keith
Lye; Milton Keynes Recycling Facility; Royal Automobile Club;
Royal Horticultural Society Library; Martin Walters; Richard
Walters; World Resources Foundation

Special thanks to Caroline Ash